Directing Your Directing Career
A Support Book and Agent Guide for Directors

© 1995 K Callan
ISBN 1-878355-01-5
ISSN 10078-2206

Other books by K Callan
An Actor's Workbook, 1986
The New York Agent Book, 1987
Second edition 1989, Third edition 1992
The Los Angeles Agent Book, Second edition 1988,
Third edition 1990, Fourth edition 1992,
Fifth edition 1994
How to Sell Yourself as an Actor, First edition 1988
Second edition 1993
The Life of the Party 1991
The Script Is Finished, Now What Do I Do?

Illustrations: Barry Wetmore
Photography: Sunny Bak
Editor: Kristi Nolte
Copy Editor: Jill Ragaway

Thank you ...

Chuck Warn of The Directors Guild of America,
Tony Blake, Florence Stanley and all the people who
return phone calls.

Table of Contents

vii	Introduction	vi
1.	Is Directing a Viable Career?	1
2.	Focus	21
3.	Are You Ready?	28
4.	Geography	37
5.	Ways into the System	47
6.	Agents, Finally	91
7.	What Everybody Wants	101
8.	The Relationship	119
9.	Star Agencies/Conglomerates	133
10	First Aid	145
11.	Researching the Agents	161
12.	Agency Listings	192
13.	Glossary	257
14.	Index to Agents	261
15	Index to Los Angeles Agents	273
16.	Index to New York Agents	281
17.	Index to Directors	283
18.	Index to Everything Else	285

Introduction

What set out to be one book about actors and agents back in 1986 has now stretched into more than ten books dealing with directors, writers and actors turning their efforts into gainful employment. The process has been very much like earning a PhD. Reading everything I can get my hands on relating to above-the-line theater and film careers has given me an invaluable overview of the business.

The most important piece of information I carry away from my studies is that most people who succeed big (or small) in show business not only have the drive, strength of character and determination to make it in a field where less than 10% in any of the guilds make over $25,000 a year, but also have a real curiosity in learning about all aspects of their job. The director who spends years observing knows he's not just waiting for his shot, but he's enjoying being there, soaking up the gravy of information and people wandering the set.

My consciousness about the business has also been dramatically raised as a result of meeting and interviewing over 300 agents in New York and Los Angeles. The process was just like every other part of the business—a learning challenge. Mostly, the agents were charming and very smart.

Regardless of the circular nature of the business and this book, my strong advice to you is to read *straight through* and not skip around. The first part provides background to critically understand the information in the latter part of the book.

If you are looking for an agent, fight the urge to run to the agency listings and read about this agent or that. Until you digest more criteria regarding the evaluating of agents, you may find yourself just as confused as before.

If you read the agents' quotes with some perception, you will gain insights not only into their character but into how the business really works. You will notice whose philosophy coincides with yours. Taken by themselves the quotes might only be interesting, but considered in context and played against the insights of other agents, they can be revealing and educational.

I've listed clients of agencies where possible, so you can see if they are your peers. Although some agencies take ads out in the trades to call attention to their lists, some of those same agents frowned on mentioning names. Most happily provided me with client lists and had me pick the names to mention, lest they leave anyone out.

Where I was unable to provide names, I've suggested checking the Directors Guild of America and Society of Stage Directors & Choreographers membership books.

Check all addresses before mailing. Every effort has been made to provide accurate and current addresses and phone numbers, but agents move and computers goof. Call the office and verify the address. They won't know it's you.

It's been a gratifying experience to come in contact with all the agents and all the other people I have met as a result of my books. Because I am asking the questions for all of us, if I've missed something you deem important, tell me and I'll include it in my next book. Write to me c/o Sweden Press, PO Box 1612, Studio City CA 91614 or via E-mail; AH497@LAFN.org.

K Callan
Los Angeles

1   Is Directing a Viable Career?

Can there be enough money to pay for the burden the director carries? He is in charge of everything. On his shoulders lie responsibility for schedule, budget, weather, food, script, actors, sets, costumes, effects, music, lighting, cinematography, the emotional climate on the set and every other single aspect of the communal project that becomes a film, television production or play.

The director is the person to whom every member of the team looks for inspiration and guidance. He's not allowed to have a bad day, the flu or a personal life while he's in charge of his producer's millions. He's expected to have all the answers or at least act like it. It's sort of like being the President. I don't know why anyone would want that job either.

More important than why someone would want to direct, however, is not just, "Is there enough money to compensate for the burden,?" but What is the feasibility of actually making a living as a director?"

Reality

Just because Steven Spielberg makes millions directing is no guarantee that you will. Spielberg is a genius, an entrepreneur, a producer, a writer and has been in the business a long time. Don't become intoxicated by the possibilities and ignore the financial realities of life as a director.

Although a career in the arts is always problematic, the life of a stage, film and/or television director can be even bleaker than for actors (29% of Screen Actors Guild members made no money at all in

1993 and only 12% made over $20,000) and writers (only 51% of the members of the Writers Guild made money in 1992 and only 10% made over $7,000).

The Directors Guild won't release their statistics. They say such data is misleading because when you average Spielberg's salary with an under-employed director, the numbers extrapolate no meaningful conclusions. There are those, however, who say the DGA releases no numbers because it's too depressing.

Right now, I would not like to be a director in this kind of market. Actors can always seem to find fringe work. They can do commercials and voiceovers or get into a play someplace. If they're absolutely down to their last dollar, they can do a play out of town. They can still earn a living or they can take another job.

Somehow when you are an actor, working in non-theatrical employment seems honorable. There's nothing wrong with waiting on tables between movies when they've got to hold their lives together. Writers can always spec something. They don't need anyone's permission to go home and write a novel or a short story, or anything for that matter, and try to get it published. They can try to earn money reporting, there are many avenues in the writing profession. But a director needs the whole apparatus of the movie business to work.

Directors cannot go home and spec out a movie shoot. They cannot spec direct something. They are higher up on the food chain; more is expected of them. And yet unemployed directors are competing head to head with major names. In a contracting market, this means the guys on the bottom and in the middle have a much harder time getting work than they would have had two years ago because the guys on the top are taking it. The guy that might have gotten a two million dollar fee four years ago is now willing to do something for a million or less

because there are fewer jobs available. This pushes everybody else down from the top and there are no other alternatives available. If you are a film or television director, it's very hard to figure, "Well, I'm going to direct a play on Melrose Avenue and industry people will come and see my work and hire me to do a movie." It just doesn't work that way.
Gary Salt
Paul Kohner, Inc.
Los Angeles

Even if The Directors Guild won't tell us much, it's not difficult to figure out that any one project can employ many writers and producers and even more actors while there is room for only one director.

█   *While the director is prepping a movie that may or may not get yanked, the writer has already finished his work and gone on to something else. The producers are (I guarantee you) developing something else simultaneously and the actors aren't on the payroll yet, but they're working for somebody else anyway. So are the other people.*
Gary Salt
The Kohner Agency
Los Angeles

To the truly driven (which one has to be to survive in the high stakes, competitive world of show business), lack of opportunity means nothing. The TDs always think numbers are for *everyone else* and don't involve them.

Even though you may feel this information does not concern you, if you want to be one of the handful who not only survive, but prosper, focusing on who works and who doesn't and why, can help strategize your plans and might even make you think again about pursuing such an ellusive livelihood. If your ardor for directing can become compromised by reality, let it. You can get on with life focusing on some other career now (instead of ten years from now) where the odds are more in your favor.

The Young White Boys Club

As in every other part of show business (and the world, why should show business be different?) the advantage belongs to young white males. To be fair, young white males have better role models and have been raised to think the world belongs to them, so they frequently initiate their own projects instead of waiting for someone else's permission and/or validation.

■ *Young males are the preferred group. It crosses a sociological line that has to do with 'life-scripting' of what happens to females when they grow up in school and males growing up in school, and who's allowed to do what. Boys growing up are allowed more freedom to explore and express and the girls aren't and this is the residual effect.*
Laya Gelff
Laya Gelff Associates
Los Angeles

The Graylist?

Although no one will say the words out loud, there is a bias against older artists in the community.

■ *Today, in Hollywood, it is not the 'Blacklist,' but the 'Graylist.' Nobody in Hollywood reveals his or her age. It goes well beyond female actresses hungry for good, mature roles. Ageism is about writers not being able to write, directors unable to direct, producers not producing. It isn't always easy to prove discrimination since people aren't likely to tell you to get lost because "you're older," any more than it's been easy to prove racial or religious discrimination.*

Some directors and writers with experience have had to grit their teeth in pitching sessions. A young executive sits stretched out at his desk facing the gray-haired writer. "So what have you done?" the exec asks. "Before or after you were born?" is the reply.

Being a star, no doubt, helps keep you off the Graylist. Mel Brooks (over 60) hasn't been affected. "I get a call a day to do something." However, he acknowledged, "if a director gets to be over 55, the studios don't call unless he has a stellar career."

Directors Guild Newsletter
September-October 1992

■ *I'm always asked, "Well, how old is this director?" It's not really ageism. They want to know all about the director. "What was he doing before?" These are viable and natural questions. The business is a young business. That's why I got out of it.*

Steve Lewis
The Directors Company
Los Angeles

Though ageism exists, older directors may just need to update their perspective. Elliot Stahler thinks chronological age isn't the issue:

■ *Everybody is looking for what's sexy. What's sexy, almost by definition, is what is new and exciting. When someone is new to the business, whether they're 20 or 50,*

---

that's sexy. Those new ideas inspire us to get the buyers excited to see the new material, someone who can take this new person and sell him to his superior. It's about what's new and exciting.

Elliot Stahler
Kaplan Stahler
Los Angeles

John Frankenheimer is 64. After a stellar career directing such classic films as *The Manchurian Candidate*, *Birdman of Alcatraz*, *Days of Wine and Roses* and *Seven Days in May*, some might think his recent work directing television movies, is evidence of ageism. Far from it. In an article in *The New York Times*, Frankenheimer says he was his own undoing:

■   *Sipping tea in his living room, Mr. Frankenheimer, tall and craggy-faced, discussed his career and Hollywood with unusual frankness. He said personal difficulties, including alcoholism, left him tormented for years and plagued his career.*

"The 1980s were spent putting my life back together," he said. "But, look, I don't want to cast myself as a victim in any way, because I'm not. I've had a terrific career and a long run. The important thing is to be resilient enough to keep stepping up to the plate. And I'm stepping up to the plate. A lot of people who make the decisions now weren't born when I was making some of my films." He shrugged and smiled, "You can't blame them. You have to do work that's good now."

"A Director Trying to Reshoot His Career"
Bernard Weinraub
The New York Times
March 24, 1994

Francis Ford Coppola has his own ideas:

Coppola doesn't believe the Hollywood lore that you lose your creativity as you get older. Instead, he says, "you can lose your confidence, you more and more start taking what you think is the way out that everyone will like. And the more you do that, the more you don't depend on what your instinct tells you to do, you can lose it—your confidence and your nerve, your ability to have faith that you'll be able to pull it off."

"Next Romance"
Rachel Abramovitz
Premiere
December 1992

Age is more of a problem in television. In film, you can be hot at any age.

Debbee Klein
Irv Schechter Company
Los Angeles

One of the joys of ageing is perspective. One of the burdens is bias. Although older artists frequently feel at the mercy of these *new young executives*, if one examines the business with perspective, they will find:

Like most areas of the arts, directing has almost always been a field in which, more often than not, artists destined for big things achieve their breakthroughs at an early age while people in other disciplines are just getting their graduate degrees or are still jockeying for a good job.

For anyone over 28, it only gets worse. A little research shows that an overwhelming number of the top directors in film history have been firmly launched on their careers by the time they were in their mid-20s. Just to offer a random sampling, those who made their first features at 25 include Ernst Lubitsch, Kenji Mizoguchi, Michael Curtiz, King Vidor, Otto Preminger, Stanley

Donen, Louis Malle, Stanley Kubrick, Wim Wenders and
Frank Capra.

"Youth Is Not Wasted on
the Young Filmmakers' Films"
Todd McCarthy
Daily Variety
February 12, 1993

The good news is that although these greats
achieved their breakthroughs at an early age, they
weren't put to death once they reached 50. Capra was
making a comeback at 60 and John Ford (whose
breakthrough was at 27) still managed to have a
distinguished 40-year career diminishing only in the
last three years of his life when he was hampered by
failing vision and a broken hip. Billy Wilder did not
start directing until he was an old man of 36 and was
still directing when he was 68. And George Abbott was
directing on Broadway when he was nearing 100 years
of age.

Whether you're directing your first film or
your 30th, and whether you're 30 or 50, if you're
successful, no one cares how old you are.

■   *And—in the sweetest irony of all for the 50-year-
old [Jan] Mr. DeBont—top studio executives all over town
are calling to offer future big budget action projects after
telling him as recently as two weeks ago that he was too
inexperienced to make such films.*

*"That's the weird thing about Hollywood, your
life can change in a day. Your life can change in two
hours. People see a movie and two hours later you can be
at the top. Or at the bottom."*

*Mr. De Bont, a Dutch-born cinematographer
whose credits include* Die Hard, Lethal Weapon 3, *and*
The Hunt for Red October, *is now savoring his sudden*

arrival at the top of the directors' list. Speed *opened over the weekend as the top box-office attraction, and many Hollywood executives and movie exhibitors are predicting that it will be in theaters through most of the summer.*

"Hurtling to the Top: A Director is Born"
Bernard Weinraub
The New York Times
June 14, 1994

Perhaps it's all physics. James Cameron was talking about Arnold Schwartzenegger's disappointing box office in *The Last Action Hero,* but he could have been discussing the career vicissitudes attributed to ageing:

I believe that everything in the universe oscillates. Everything is a wave. It's quantum physics. Everything goes back and forth. Tide goes in, tide goes out—Arnold had been surfing that tide for a long time. Tide went back out. Hopefully it will be coming back on my movie.*
Lasting Impact
Joshua Mooney
Movieline
July 1994

* *True Lies.* It did.

Writer-director Paul Schrader was a busy director in the 1970s. The director of *American Gigolo, Light Sleeper, Blue Collar* and *Hard Core,* he wrote the screenplays for *Taxi Driver, Raging Bull* and *The Last Temptation of Christ.* His tide has been out for a while and he has taken it into his hands to bring it back in:

Ever since I left Los Angeles, which is about 12 years ago now, I've been doing these relatively personal films, on a smaller and smaller scale. It's been getting harder and harder for me to raise money. It just occurred to me this year that I had been away too long and there was a whole generation of young executives who never had met me personally, who didn't know what I was like.

They simply associate me with the D-word, which is the current curse word, "dark." So that ends any conversation. If you want to dismiss a film, an actor, a director, a writer—out of hand, in a meeting—all you say is "He's dark". Then they move on to another subject. Conversation ended, so I had to do something that got me out of that pigeonhole.

"Exorcising His Dark Side"
Daniel Cerone
The Los Angeles Times
August 13, 1994

Minorities and Women

As difficult as it is for those over 40 to find work, being a minority and/or a woman stacks the deck even further. There's no old boy network to mentor you and there are few role models to emulate. Minorities and women have not been allowed inside the castle walls long enough to help those on the outside. Things are better now, but they have a long way to go:

It's easier for women now than it ever has been. There are more jobs open to them in the industry. They are requesting black women directors.

Rima Greer
Above the Line Agency
Los Angeles

I believe it's been demonstrated that it is harder to get work for women as directors. At least historically,

---

that's certainly been true. I think there have been changes in the last few years, but still, it's been more difficult for women.

Jim Preminger
Jim Preminger Agency
Los Angeles

While the DGA won't publish numbers relative to earnings of members at large, they recently published a ten-year study that discusses employment for the women and minorities within their membership that was detailed in *The Hollywood Reporter*:

■ *The report, which looked at employment figures from 1983-93, found that in many job categories there was little or no improvement in the employment of women and minorities over the past eleven years. The report updates a study released two years ago that found similar results in employment numbers for the years 1983-91.*

"The figures for the period 1983 through 1993 reveal a woeful record of employment for DGA women and minorities," said Warren Adler, the DGA's western executive secretary and affirmative action officer.

The report shows that of all the days worked by DGA directors last year, only 7% went to female directors and that less than 4% went to ethnic minority directors. That's actually lower than the numbers in several previous years. Ten per cent of the Guild's 5,645 directors are female; sixteen are black, five are Hispanic, nine are Oriental . *

"DGA: Hiring of Minorities,
Women, Woeful, Bleak."
David Robb
The Hollywood Reporter
May 20-22, 1994

* The DGA membership also includes assistant directors, second assistant directors and unit production managers.

Jesus Treviño reacted to the original study:

█   *The DGA report covers the period 1983-1991...the only area that marked improvement was directing, growing from 1% of days worked in 1983 to 1.3% of days worked in 1991. An increase of one-third of a percent a decade! With progress being measured at a third of a percent per decade, Latinos can expect something approaching parity with their national population by the year 2282 A.D.—nearly 300 years from now.*
  What is astounding is that while employment opportunities for non-minority women have improved ever so gradually, the situation for Latinos, with but one exception, has gotten worse over the last decade. While a handful of us have managed to achieve some level of success, the overall message the industry is sending to us is quite clear, "Latinos need not apply: The American Dream is not for Latinos."

"Looking Beyond the Statistics"
Jesus Salvador Treviño
DGA News
June-July 1992

An article in *The New York Times* pointed out the breadth of the struggle for women:

█   *The struggle of white women directors has been going on at least since the Silent Era, when Mabel Normand directed Mack Sennett shorts. But only in the late 1970s and early '80s, when women like Claudia Weill and Martha Coolidge started directing mainstream movies, did Hollywood begin to appear receptive. More*

recently, the ranks of women directors have expanded to include prominent names like Penny Marshall, Barbra Streisand, Jodie Foster and Nora Ephron.
"On the Outside, Looking In"
Bronwen Hruska/Graham Rayman
The New York Times
February 21, 1993

■ *When asked if she believes Hollywood is finally ripe for more women of mettle behind the lens, Julie Cypher (director of* Teresa's Tattoo) *doesn't skip a beat. "It's not about male or female. It's about whether or not you can do the job and I can't believe that I'm the only person who thinks that." Cypher feels strongly that being a woman hasn't impeded her ascent up the slippery rungs of the Hollywood ladder. "I mean, even those good ol' boys who sit up in their big black towers, they gotta go, 'Is this a person who's gonna make me some money? Are they gonna do a good job on this film?' And that's all they care about. That's gotta be it. I hope so anyway."*
"Julie Cypher Tattoos Hollywood"
Dawn Ritchie
CineNews
First Quarter, 1994

Good News/Bad News

As with all adversity, people who win are the ones who turn it around and make it work for them:

■ *In some ways, the difficulty women had in moving into corporate circles was a boon for those with entrepreneurial spirits. If they couldn't play with the big boys, then they'd make their own game. They formed their own production companies and, in so doing, created their own niche, led by the likes of Marcy Carsey, Diane*

English, Carol Black and Linda Bloodworth-Thomason.
"Beyond Barriers"
Roberta G. Wax
EMMY/October 1994

■ *Though it is difficult for any film maker to break
into Hollywood, it is especially hard for black women,
who face not only problems of financing, distribution and
access, but also what they perceive as a paralyzing
combination of institutional racism and sexism.*
"On the Outside, Looking In"
Bronwen Hruska/Graham Rayman
The New York Times
February 21, 1993

■ *If you are a minority, you have to be three times
as good as anyone, but if you are, you'll work forever.*
Rima Greer
Above the Line Agency
Los Angeles

Terri McCoy is one of the 16 black women
directors in The Directors Guild. She worked on
television's *In Living Color.*

■ *I pretty much came up through the ranks, from
production assistant to script supervisor to stage manager,
assistant director, and finally director. Hopefully things
are changing, but not fast enough. You've got women who
work in episodic TV, women who do features, documentaries, soaps, news, but in terms of non-sitcom, not-
episodic, there's hardly anybody out there.*
"Women's Work"
Rip Reese
EMMY /October 1992

The New York Times pinpoints the reason why:

■   *...[black women] may have found more
opportunity in television than in film because blacks
make up about 25 percent of the prime-time audience, but
only 10 percent of the movie-going audience. Also, a
Federal Communications Commission affirmative action
policy requires television stations to actively recruit
minority employees. The regulations do not apply to the
film industry.*
  "On the Outside, Looking In"
  Bronwen Hruska/Graham Rayman
  The New York Times
  February 21, 1993

■   *Racism is still rampant within Hollywood,
especially when it comes to hiring minorities for key
executive posts. But there are indications that some
studio chiefs are starting mandates to add more women
and minorities.*
  *"The primary focus for black performers is
still comedy...but behind the scenes, less than 2% of
producers, directors and writers are black," according to
Sandra J. Evers-Manly, president of the Beverly
Hills/Hollywood NAACP.*
  *She added that "The Beverly Hills/Hollywood
chapter of the NAACP has now turned its efforts toward
helping its members get funding to do their own short
films...We've got to diversify our crafts and help people
get their start at writing and directing and producing,"
she said.*
  "Minority Hiring Lags"
  Kathleen O'Steen
  Daily Variety
  February 19, 1993

Susan Schulman agrees with Rima Greer that women must achieve more than men to be accepted:

Directing is still thought of as a man's job, and, as they say, 'A woman has to be twice as good to get half as far.' I can't tell you the number of times the comment has been made about me, especially if I'm directing a musical—"It's an awfully' big' production, do you think you can handle it?" I know that I'm small and that doesn't help. True, I'm getting fewer comments like that because I'm known now. But the fact is, if I were a man with identical credentials, that kind of comment would not be made.

"Inside the Secret Garden"
Simi Horwitz
TheaterWeek
February 10-16, 1992

Spike Lee, Robert Townsend and John Singleton are all contenders these days. These men not only wrote and directed their first films, but in most cases raised the money as well. Robert Townsend, who wrote and directed *Hollywood Shuffle*, has become a show business legend because he financed that successful first film with credit card advances.

Robert Rodriguez was twenty-four when he wrote, directed and produced *El Mariachi*. An innovative entrepreneur, he not only managed to make his first feature for $7,000, but raised money by participating in medical experiments and landed CAA as his agent. He wrote the script while lying in bed hospitalized for the tests. He even cast from the hospital bed, choosing a fellow guinea pig for the film.

Because the public is unaccustomed to seeing people of color at all, these examples appear to be great progress. And they are. But they still represent a very small percentage of the overall pie.

Lest anyone jump to the conclusion that higher black employment has anything to do with affirmative action, talent or fairness, let's be clear: higher black employment reflects the growing economic clout of the black community. The only way other minorities are going to find work in the marketplace is by finding innovative ways to finance their projects.

Twenty women, age 18-23, were all desperately seeking to break into filmmaking. So they took out a full-page ad in the May 13 issue of Entertainment Weekly *that read, "Please, please, please, please, please, can we have some money to finish our film? Before you say no, picture this: Twenty ethnically diverse young women with vision, passion and absolutely no money." Just two months after the ad ran (donated by the magazine), they were on location with a $25,000 budget and a nine-day shooting schedule.*

"Breaking Into the Boys' Club"
Anne Bergman
The Los Angeles Times
August 26, 1994

Graciela Daniele, the Tony Award-nominated director of the recently closed hit musical, Once on an Island, *doesn't believe that Broadway is sexist, but "fearful of anything new and untried." The financial stakes are enormous. Women directors are largely new and untried.*

"Women Directors Make
Inroads on Broadway"
Simi Horwitz
TheaterWeek
February 10-16, 1992

Minorities must have the motivation and the

vision to tear down the barriers standing in their way. Money and success come to those who pursue it and believe they deserve it. I don't blame the white male establishment: it is their money, they get to tell any story they want. As minorities learn to raise money, they will be able to tell stories about people who are not white men under 50. Julianne Boyd, executive vice-president of the Society of Stage Directors and Choreographers echoes the importance of being entrepreneurial:

Women directors could also make it to Broadway by conceiving their own projects—preferably musicals—from scratch and presenting them somewhere else. I did it with Eubie, *Liz Swados did it with* Runaways *in the 70s. The point is, there had to be evidence that it was a money-making project elsewhere.*

"Inside the Secret Garden"
Simi Horwitz
TheaterWeek
February 10-16, 1992

According to producer Gale Ann Hurd (*The Terminator, Aliens,* etc.*),* not everybody discriminates:

The interesting thing about working for Roger [Corman] was that it was not like the rest of Hollywood: women had an equal chance to do anything. It was complete equal-opportunity exploitation. You had an opportunity to do anything. Roger believed in you more than you did. That's so rare. It changed my life.

"A Woman Who Knows What Men Like: Action Films"
Bernard Weinraub
The New York Times
May 3, 1994

Walt Disney Studios head and Academy of Television Arts & Sciences President, Rich Frank, makes the best point of all. He's talking about women, but his words are true for all the minorities:

Maybe the men on the ladder are on higher rungs, not because there are some rungs missing for women, but because the guys started on the ladder earlier and have been climbing longer. There's nothing holding [anyone] down, just time, and each day that erodes a little bit.
"Breaking Barriers"
Roberta G. Wax
EMMY/October 1994

A director is the driving force behind someone's large financial investment. When management sees that you have been willing to either raise your own money or spend your own money, that goes a long way toward building credibility for you as a product. When I found out someone else was willing to invest in my first book, I decided to publish it myself. Money equals credibility in the marketplace. Why should show business be different? The way that anyone makes inroads into the business is when he stops waiting to be chosen.

I'd Really Rather Direct

Even if you are a white thirty-something-year-old male making money as a director, it's a tough business. Not only do you have as competition all the people in the world who started out with directing as their goal, but also writers disenchanted with directors' vision of their work, actors who want to be more powerful and producers who have already done everything else. These people are probably already more connected than you, with better avenues of access into the business. If you are still determined to reinvent the wheel, read on. For those with drive, wit, vision, ego and a masochistic outlook, there is always room.

Wrap Up

Career as a Director
financial outlook bleak
monumental responsibility
great stature
get power and respect
less opportunity for work than writers and actors
masochistic persona helpful

Age
young white men get the work
age is not necessarily chronological
box office is the bottom line

Women and Minorities
work much less
less opportunity to make money
must be entrepreneurial
have no old boy network
need to initiate their own projects
need to raise their own money

2   Focus

Even though you may think you can direct anything anywhere, the peculiarities of the marketplace demand that you choose an area of the business and make it your own. Gone are the days when being a director meant either film or theater.

In film there's action, drama, adventure, comedy, fantasy, documentary, animation, science fiction, horror, commercials (with all their categories), etc. In television there are even more alternatives: situation comedies, daytime soaps, nighttime soaps, drama, reality, sporting events, award shows, MTV, news shows, interactive television, game shows; the list goes on and on. Theater runs the gamut from one-person shows to extravagant musicals.

It doesn't matter if you are talented enough to be successful in every area. You will be pigeon-holed by someone else if you don't do it yourself, so make a decision and then explore the marketplace.

Pick an area and focus on it. A smart business person researches his marketplace. He finds out what is already available and checks to see how his product compares in quality, price and style to other products already for sale. His product needs to be trend setting or so perfectly in tune with an existing product, that he could go to that employer and expect to be hired instantly. Surely you have done this homework already—or don't you consider your directing career to be a business?

Although you may be anxious to find an agent, your next step is to develop your product. You must hone your craft to a particular niche in the market-place; not the hot niche, but your niche. It means exploring your own strengths and weaknesses in order to determine what you bring to varying material:

■ *A director is much more dependent on the long term than the short term. He must turn down the work that is not going to take him forward on his journey. A director has very few short term advantages if it's a direction he doesn't want to go. Taking a job for money can close off opportunities for the director because it can type you very badly.*
  Barry Douglas
  DGRW
  New York

■ *How a director uses the artistic skills available to him depends a lot on his temperament...how he sees everything, what he sees...not solely on how he conceptualizes his movie. I know a director who has an inherent taste for violence; he notices the slightest indication of a violent nature or a violent act...the fingers on a hand, writhing for contact with a jaw..a stuntman playfully grabbing a fella's head over his shoulder and running that head toward a hanging pot. He notices these things in his daily life and on the set; and that director is damn good at violent action pictures.*
  However, I know another director whose inclination is to turn his head away from the bloody brutality of a cat overtaking a mouse, jaws open; that director won't see nor imagine the violent actions that will make a violence-oriented picture better. On the other hand, this same director can direct soft material and never let it get sloppy, saccharine; he sees the soft gesture...the little token of affection...on the set or in daily life. Both these men, the harsh and the gentle, have stored up devices within themselves to portray what your screenplay, whichever way it tends, better.
  So directors are artists, and as such, are the result

of their persona, shaped by their life experiences.
What a Producer Does
Buck Hougton
Sillman James Press 1991

■ *I think that what's critical in each case is to find
out what someone is best suited for and to make that
choice. If someone is a born film director, then it's going to
be harder to get him started in television than it is in film.
It just depends. I'm surprised at the level of self-awareness
that a lot of people have and also at the level of flexibility
that they exhibit. We have some people who are primarily
motion picture directors and that's their real interest, but
they are delighted to get work in television as a first step.*
Jim Preminger
Jim Preminger Agency
Los Angeles

■ *You need to have a career plan. You should have a
one-year plan, and a two-year plan and a five-year plan.
Where do you want to be in five years? Then start doing
all the things that you need to do to create that career.*
*If you ultimately want to do film, I think you
should start out in film and develop those kinds of
relationships with people that will lead you to that film
goal. Talk to and work with and observe some of the top
film directors in not only television movies and episodic
and pilots, but also features. That involves a lot of foot-
work on the directors' part. This town is based on
relationships. It's based on who is the director 'du jour.'*
*If you can get some kind of groundswell of
support and people talking about you as well as some real
experience at knowing the technical end of it, I think that
when you finally get your shot, your career will be in
better shape. The focus and plan is very important. That
changes every year. You may fall into something that you*

love doing. If you just go about saying: "I want to be a director" without knowing what it is you want to do, you waste a lot of time.

Stephen Rose
Major Clients Agency
Los Angeles

For theater directors much more than actors, you have to stake out your own territory and fulfill it because you have nothing else to prove what you can do.

Barry Douglas
DGRW
New York

I believe in focus. When people are good at too many things, they end up hurting themselves very often. The clients of mine that are the most successful are the ones that are very focused.

Michele Wallerstein
Wallerstein Kappleman
Los Angeles

Associations make everything. There are different kinds of careers and you need to understand very early in your professional life that this business boxes directors in even more than actors because people are more insecure because there is so much money at stake. Directors have less chance to prove their range and their focus than an actor. An actor can give you an audition, a director can't. He is only judged by what he's done before. If everything he's done is a 1950s musical at a second-rate stock house, no one is going to trust him with a first-rate idea.

Depending on where you want to go, a lot of people who get into the regional get typed as regional directors, i.e. they cannot create a piece, they can only do classics. They make the most of the economies, but not *necessarily the art of directing. Someone who has a number of successful revivals in major regional houses might still take a backseat to someone who will do a new play in a 70-seat house off-off-off Broadway in New York where it is accessible to someone who could do something with it or the new play has a voice that can be sent out. If the writer will attach you to it, that's also a better journey. There are indeed different paths depending on what your own strengths are.*

> Barry Douglas
> *DGRW*
> New York

Once you have isolated your field of vision, focus your research in that area. Who is working in that venue? How did they get started? Did they attend film school? Spend time observing? Produce a short film? Attend festivals? Write their own material? Did they amass a body of work in their hometown before going to New York or Los Angeles or Chicago?

An inspiring article entitled *Elia Kazan: On What Makes a Director,* which appeared in the *DGA Newsletter* in the January 1990 issue details the strengths and talents needed to be a first-rate film director. If you are a DGA member, you may already have read it. If not, I'd certainly visit the *DGA Newsletter* archives or visit the library of the Academy of Motion Picture Arts and Sciences at 333 South La Cienega in Beverly Hills in order to read it. The Motion Picture Arts and Sciences library is, by the way, an invaluable resource if you live in Los Angeles. If you don't live in Los Angeles, back copies of *The DGA Newsletter* can be ordered. Their phone number is 310-247-3020.

Stop Waiting Around

If you want to direct, get on with it. If no one will pay you to direct, gather actors and writers into a collective and direct for free. Think of it as graduate school without the fee, for as surely as night follows day, practice makes product. You and your actors and writers can bring forth a powerful synergistic product that will command both attention and respect. If you keep doing the work, someone will find you.

Woody Allen, John Cassavettes and Spike Lee are just a few of the entrepreneurs who didn't wait to be validated by someone else. When you look at the progression of their films, it's easier to see why the mainstream marketplace wasn't eager to bankroll their efforts. But as they developed, the money appeared. Stop waiting.

Commitment

Being able to do everything in the business doesn't necessarily mean you should *do* everything. Chairman of New World Entertainment, Brandon Tartikoff cited the importance of career focus:

There's nothing like cancer to get you focused on what's important. The first time around, I just felt that I had this bad card dealt to me. I was in my mid-20s, tre- mendously cocky, and what the illness did was bring a humility to the situation. I'm not saying that I'm a poster boy for humility right now, but it changed me. With no bad card dealt, I might have become a reasonably successful local television manager. I had 18 balls in the air— acting at the Second City Workshop in Chicago, writing plays, writing free-lance articles for The New Times Magazine.

Afterward, I just focused. You know you're sick, and you've got to do this and that to try to get the result you want, and you put on blinders and plunge right ahead. I definitely bought into the concept that the cancer was curable and to look ahead this year and next year.

"Tartikoff Examines"
Bernard Weinraub
The New York Times
October 13, 1992

Tartikoff's words make a big impression. It is advantageous to learn all aspects of the business in order to choose our specialties but, having too many balls in the air may prevent our dreams from coming true.

You really cannot have everything. Nobody has it all. It's like going into a room with the best food in the world. You can put it all on your plate, if you want, but you can't possibly consume it all without becoming sick. You can have a taste of many things or you can choose your favorite and make a meal of it.

Wrap Up

Define Your Goals
pick your genre and stick to it
study the marketplace
find your niche
collaborate
keep directing
keep networking
decide what is important to you
focus

3   Are You Ready?

There are no shortcuts into the system. You don't
write a query letter to become a member of an
Olympic team. There are maybe 300 people
representing our country at that level. Training,
practice, pain, no personal life, nerve and dedication
are the basic qualifications. Talent is a given. How
many directing members of the DGA do you suppose
make a livable wage? I'm sure it's on a par with the
number of members of the Olympic teams.

If you begin with the preliminaries and develop
your career in an orderly fashion, you are making
friends and fans along the way. They are watching
your development and waiting for your abilities to
bring you to the Olympics. You can only get there by
demonstrating a pattern of excellence and health every
step of the way. A student film from a connected film
school or a dossier of important credits in respected
theater venues is only the beginning.

You're Only a Virgin Once

Before you begin working your way into the system,
it is imperative that you are *ready* to be judged. You
are only new once. Even if you have a film can under
your arm holding a prize-winning student film, that is
only the first step. You are only ready when you can
orchestrate the next move *after* you have the industry's attention.

■   *Along with your great short film or your great
one million-dollar feature, have a script that's reasonable
for you to direct whether you wrote it or your friend wrote*

it and you have $100 on it.
Rima Greer
Above the Line Agency
Los Angeles

Young directors think they are ready for an agent before they are. They need a body of work even if it's small. To be out of film school with only one film is not enough. How I do know that you're not a flash in the pan? Have they ever directed a play? Go do some waiver theater. Learn about actors.

I don't know that I would take a new director with just one little film unless it was big enough and special enough. Try and get commercials or an industrial. Do some MTV. Nothing is easy. So many people think that they deserve it before they deserve it, whether it's actors or writers or directors. They think that because they've written one script or directed one college film that they are ready for an agent and ready for the studios. They're not. Get some experience. Do some waiver theater. People will come see you. They will.
Michele Wallerstein
Wallerstein Kappleman
Los Angeles

A director needs one good strong piece of film coupled with material that, preferably, he has written himself. Everybody wants to be in business with a writer-director. If you have material and film that clearly shows talent and ability, then you have a lot to work with.
Michael Douroux
Douroux & Co.
Los Angeles

It's incumbent upon the director to have some material so that when you get to the point where you have

---

somebody's attention, you can tell them what you want to do. The director needs a portfolio of things he wants to do.
Martin Shapiro
Shapiro-Lichtman
Los Angeles

■ *Everyone has his own pace. I wanted to have a film credit by the time I was 30. I was nine years late. I would encourage anyone who wants to direct to learn everything he can about the nuts and bolts of filmmaking. It isn't all just about making a cool shot and learning about lenses. It's about "What do you do when you arrive on the set and the trucks are parked in the wrong place and you don't have time to move them?" That's a skill that comes from a lot of experience. The other thing I'm learning is that performance is everything. It isn't about the camera although it's always better to try to tell the story visually or enhance the story visually. Much of my preparation time is spent in figuring out how to tell the story visually, but what it really comes down to is "What kind of actor are you going to hire?" and "How are you going to get the performance out of him?"*
John Kretchmer/*Director*

Career Plans

Julie Cypher is a good example of someone with an overall career plan, whether or not she wrote it down on paper. As a Radio, TV and Film major at the University of Texas, she worked at local television stations. When she graduated she came to Los Angeles and worked as a production assistant, then as a second assistant director and then as 1st AD.

She did all the things you're supposed to do: got herself trained, began working in the business doing whatever she could, formed relationships, nurtured them, wrote her own material and then put up her own money to produce her calling card reel which she took to festivals. During all this time, her eye was alert for material.

She knew she wanted a light comedy, "nothing too heavy." Her material came to her through a relationship she formed at an industry support group, *Cinewomen*. After she optioned the material, it still took her two-and-a-half years to get it made:

■ *In Hollywood, first-time directors are a risk few studios wish to assume and Julie was no exception. Armed with a healthy resume boasting directorial credits on numerous music videos and AD gigs on features, Cypher still had never helmed a full-length feature herself. Sensing what she was up against, Cypher first produced a 35mm short film as a calling card reel to show. Recruiting friends for roles, Julie lined up Hollywood hot-tickets such as Dermott Mulroney, k.d. lang, comedienne Ellen DeGeneres, singer Melissa Etheridge and former husband Lou Diamond Phillips* to populate her cast. Ardous Moon *which Cypher wrote and directed, eventually played the film festival circuit. "It served its purpose very well," Cypher claims, "and it was a lot of fun."*

Reel and script in hand, Cypher immediately began hustling financing for Teresa's Tattoo. *"I just started knocking on doors trying to get people to trust me with a million and a half dollars." Eventually she approached director Marc Rocco, half of the Marc Rocco-Phil McKeon directing/producing team which made* Where the Day Takes You *for Yankee Entertainment Group.*

"Julie Cypher Tattoos Hollywood"
Dawn Ritchie
CineNews
First Quarter, 1994

■   *Let's say you have a film that you have directed
and it's generally regarded to be pretty good. There are a
zillion directors around who have credits down to the
floor. Why is somebody going to want to hire you? If you
have a screenplay that people are falling down about, you
can say, "This is my screenplay. I own it. I have it under
option. If you want to make this movie, it's gotta be me.
It's not going to be Joe Sargent or whomever." It's
leverage. You have to have something they want.*
      Stu Robinson
      paradigm
      Los Angeles

■   *The problem with the director is that if the career
is so spectacular that it's won awards and created
attention, then maybe there's a job someplace for the
director that someone is willing to give him. More often
than not, what happens with the reel is somebody says,
"This director is very talented. What does he or she
want to do?"*
      Marty Shapiro
      Shapiro-Lichtman
      Los Angeles

■   *Darnell Martin (*I Like It Like That*), a graduate
student at the Tisch School of the Arts at New York
University, played her cards perfectly last year. When her
thesis film was shown at the school's annual screenings
and attracted the interest of Spike Lee, Ms. Martin had a
120-page script ready to show. Mr. Lee read it, liked it and
bought it. He would serve as executive producer for the
film for Universal Pictures, with Ms. Martin directing.*
      "So, You Wanna Be a Director"
      William Grimes
      The New York Times
      January 17, 1993

■ *Besides having a great film, you better have a great script under your arm, or if you are a theater director, you'd better have an impressive resume and a great script.*

Rima Greer
Above the Line Agency
Los Angeles

■ *The new person...should try to meet and cultivate people. Try to find material that he wants to do. It's very tough for a new director. It's tough for a new writer, too, but a new writer can write 10 scripts and maybe the 10th one will work. A new director can't go out and direct 10 short films and maybe the 10th one will work. With the writer, all you are dealing with is time and whatever it costs per page for paper and the computer. The director can't do that. Unless the director's film is really out-standing, the director has got to find some other way in; maybe it's being a producer and finding a property. If the director is a writer, then he can write his own material.*

Marty Shapiro
Shapiro-Lichtman
Los Angeles

Steve Lewis runs an agency that specializes in directors:

■ *There's less work so it's more competitive and it's tougher to get a break. It's like the door shut four or five years ago. People should have their dreams and hope, but lower their expectations and lengthen their time frames.*

Steve Lewis
The Directors Company
Los Angeles

Career Progression

It's human nature: once an artist makes inroads in one area, he wants to move to another. If he was successful in commercials, the goal becomes television, if he was successful in television, now he's looking for a feature. If you are trying to make that progression, patience can spell the difference in whether you ever get another shot:

What happens usually is that very successful television directors say, "This isn't enough. I want to be Steven Spielberg." They get antsy very quickly and in order to meet that need and keep the client, the agent may jump too hastily. I think that's sort of convenient for the agency as well.

If a client is making millions of dollars as a television director, for his first feature, he's not going to make that much money and it's going to take a year. The agency knows they're not going to make money, so I don't think there is a sincere desire for the director to succeed.

If the director fails, he will go back to doing what has made the agency so much money in the first place. It's sort of a Catch-22. As far as I am concerned, you either do it right, or you don't do it.
Stephen Rose
Major Clients Agency
Los Angeles

Because Hollywood overproduces actors, writers, directors and all the other components necessary to make films, only those with a game plan to go along with their talent will prevail. You have probably worked your fingers to the bone not only directing your film, but possibly raising the money and building the sets. Even if your film makes you *hot* for a few moments, that's all it will be unless you are prepared with a follow-up.

Even if you can get CAA to look at your reel and be excited about you, if you can't demonstrate to them how they can sell you, their ardor will cool quickly.

Subject Matter

As a member of the Academy of Motion Picture Arts and Sciences, I am not only privileged to judge the Academy Awards, but also those films entered into student film competitions. Although there are films of social significance and short films based on classical short stories (since they're in the public domain) and polemics that stir the feelings on some level, the consistent winners are those that tell their stories with humor. If you are choosing material, don't use the opportunity to pay your family back for early trauma, unless you can be hilarious doing it.

Most people, civilians and industry people alike cannot separate out the material from the work, so if you want people to choose you, remember that. I asked agents if they were able to look past material to the talent of the director:

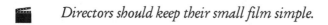 *I doubt that I would have that much zeal. I'd have to have a film that pretty much can tell anybody that this is a talented person. The storyline doesn't have to be complicated or deep. We've scored with some directors because it was arresting and fast moving.*
Stu Robinson
paradigm
Los Angeles

Directors should keep their small film simple.

They have a tendency to clutter things up. Keep it simple and honest. There's a certain focus that hits the camera. Whether it's a character study or a small story, it doesn't lose its specialness if they don't clutter it up.

Michele Wallerstein
Wallerstein Kappleman
Los Angeles

When someone does a short film, I think they should pick a mini-mini movie, something that has some commercial appeal. One of the problems is that the young people who go to school or raise $10,000 or get a grant, pick a play of some sort, an old Ibsen classic or The House of Bernado Alba. *Not that they can't do a good job, but they're self-indulgent. In today's market, they could do a mini-mini movie that would be very commercial. They could do eight or ten minutes, it doesn't matter; you could hook somebody who would then say, "I want to work with that person."*

Marty Shapiro
Shapiro-Lichtman
Los Angeles

Being ready is so important that I have taken a whole chapter to make the point. Agents, producers, readers, and studio executives have all told me that being prepared for the second step is even more important than being ready for the first step.

Wrap Up

Be Prepared
know what you want to do next
have a good commercial script in your control
have a career plan
if you are trying to change categories, be patient

4   Geography

Whatever your directing focus, there's work to be
done no matter where you live. If your home town is
so small that there is no theater group, start one and
begin at once to direct. When I asked agents the first
thing a director should do when he got off the bus, I
was surprised when a couple laughed and said, *get back
on.* They were joking, but there is wisdom behind
the joke.

Is there a way to make a living as a director if
you are not living in one of the big media centers? Of
course there is. Most cities have some kind of local
television producing facilities as well as some kind of
film company that puts together commercials for the
local banks and utility companies. Once you begin
your research, you will probably find that there is
some small production company that shoots local
educational and/or industrial films (see Glossary). I'm
not saying you'll make a mint doing it, but, hey, you
may not make a mint doing it in Los Angeles or New
York either. If you stay in your own hometown, you
will probably have a lower overhead, more prestige
and the ability to have Sunday dinner with Mom. Not
only that, surely you already know people and can
forge a support group of lifelong acquaintances. On the
other hand, all of the above reasons may be the very
things propelling you to leave Kansas.

If local businesses don't have a hometown
outlet for their commercials, perhaps it's time they did
and you can become the big hero who teaches them
how to do that. Maybe the comics at your local
comedy club would love to have you put all their work
onto a comedy reel for them to send to agents and/or
clubs in New York or Los Angeles. If you put together
an imaginative reel, this is a chance for your work to

get some attention, too.

Befriend anyone in town who wants to write and encourage them to write a play or a film. Stage their work or film it. You'll both begin to acquire fans, and who knows? Perhaps your admirers will have money to finance your projects.

Susan Schulman, director of *The Secret Garden*, got her break on Broadway by giving up on ever getting a chance in New York:

I almost threw in the towel. I had come to terms with the fact that I might never direct a Broadway play. At that point, I wasn't even sure I'd direct a commercial off-Broadway play. But then after a lot of soul-searching, I decided that even if I never made it commercially in New York, I could still make a living elsewhere doing what I loved to do.

Once I accepted the fact that I might not work on Broadway, a big weight was lifted from me. I suddenly felt freer to take theatrical risks. And perhaps that even opened doors for me.

"Inside the Secret Garden"
Simi Horwitz
TheaterWeek
February 10-16, 1992

Susan is one of many women who have experienced first hand the sexism involved in theater.

When Susan Schulman applied to Yale's School of Drama as a directing major 24 years ago, she was rejected on the grounds that the school "hasn't had much luck with women directors," recalls Schulman. Manhattan Theater Club artistic director Lynn Meadow was told the same thing by Yale.

"They didn't want to invest the time and money

---

training a woman who, in their view," Schulman
continues, *"would get married, ultimately have a family
and drop out of the profession."*
"Inside the Secret Garden"
Simi Horwitz
TheaterWeek
February 10-16, 1992

Certainly this thinking has been responsible
for the number of women who have been more
successful creating careers for themselves outside the
major marketplaces.

■ *"Although women directors, especially on
Broadway, are still a rare breed, there are more of us than
ever before," says Julianne Boyd, executive director of the
Society of Stage Directors and Choreographers. "Twenty
percent of the membership are women and fifty percent of
the board of directors are women. But most are practicing
their craft in regional theaters across the country and off-
Broadway as opposed to Broadway."*
"On the Outside, Looking In"
Bronwen Hruska/Graham Rayman
The New York Times
February 21, 1993

There are varying reasons to stay in another
environment until Hollywood or New York beckons:

■ *Roger Donaldson, director of* The Getaway, *lives
year-round in the States, but believes it's best to wait to
come to the U.S. after one has made his or her name as a
filmmaker at home. "The only way you're going to break
into Hollywood is to be asked to come here, and to get in
this door, you need a film that has some critical or
financial success," said Donaldson, whose film* Smash

Palace *brought him to Hollywood's attention in 1981. "If given the opportunity to come here, don't turn it down, but don't come with too many expectations because it's pretty tough. A director needs to be a tough businessman to survive in Hollywood."*

"Directors Down Under"
Mary Hardesty
DGA News
Dec 93-Jan 94

It's possible that you'll decide to stay in Des Moines, Dallas, Hot Springs or even Australia. If you do decide to leave, however, all the things you do at home are the same things you'll need to do in Los Angeles; just on a bigger scale. Check out the marketplace, see who is working, how they got there, how to do it better, differently or more economically and then start doing it. There is always a way.

New York/Los Angeles/Chicago/Atlanta/Etc.

Whereas New York remains the center for directing for the theater and Los Angeles for film and television, there are viable venues in Minneapolis, San Francisco and Chicago for theater directors and Atlanta, Chicago and Florida for film and television directors. Although more and more filming takes place in these locales, most of the hiring is done in Los Angeles or New York unless the production originates locally. TNT television does several series in Florida and the series *Seaquest* has just moved to Florida in order to avoid union crews and cut costs.

Though there is work in these areas, the directors are usually hired out of Los Angeles. I've worked with many prominent directors who now live in Arizona or Colorado or Montana, but they established their careers in Los Angeles. Once you are known, you can leave, but if you want to make it as an important film director, you'd better plan on moving to Los Angeles. Although states like Florida and Texas with tough anti-union stances lure filmmakers, these locales lack the components to really compete.

Paul Lazarus, the director of the motion picture program at the University of Miami, was quoted in *The New York Times* regarding the number of recent films (*True Lies, Ace Ventura: Pet Detective, Drop Zone, The Specialist*) that lensed in Miami:

■ *For the moment, it is a congenial place to make pictures, like Santa Fe is and like Texas was. Some of that will inevitably disappear when the heat on South Florida and Miami Beach goes away. You don't stay white-hot as a destination point for the indeterminate future. We're not ever, in my lifetime, becoming competitive with Los Angeles, and probably not with New York. The problem is a lack of local talent that forces movie makers to import workers from Hollywood. What have you got in Florida? You have no creative community. Yes, you can crew up a major picture in terms of grips and gaffers, but where are our directors? Where are our leading actors, our producers, our cinematographers?*

"Miami, the Whatever-You-Care-to-Name-It of Florida"
Vernon Silver
The New York Times
August 14, 1994

Michael Pattinson is developing *Horn of Africa* for Michael Douglas' Stonebridge Productions:

■ *I found that what was impeding me from getting my projects off the ground was not being in Hollywood.*

You need to be here to take meetings and field offers. I think I would be frustrating my agent's efforts on my behalf if I wasn't living here.
"Directors Down Under"
Mary Hardesty
DGA News
Dec 93-Jan 94

The prize-winning student film of New York director, Tamara Jenkins put her name at the top of Los Angeles agents' *gotta see* lists. Even though she was in demand, it became clear that you'd better live in Los Angeles if you expect to get work:

■ *... Then, if they are interested, they want to see a feature script. Then, they want to know whether you're moving to L.A. They try to convince you that you can't make a movie unless you're in L.A. It's spooky.*
"So, You Wanna Be a Movie Director?"
William Grimes
The New York Times
January 17, 1993

Director Rod Hardy came to Hollywood with 450 hours of Australian television credits to his name:

■ *"If you have a product to sell, you might as well come to the biggest marketplace. But coming here as an almost unknown was a big risk. It was very hard for me to get that first job,"* recalled Hardy, who has lived in Los Angeles for three years and spent the first year-and-a-half doing the get-to-know-you-meeting *runs.*
"Directors down Under"
Mary Hardesty
DGA News
Dec 93-Jan 94

Make a Home for Yourself

If you do leave your roots for a new city, one of the most important things you can do for yourself is put together a cozy, light place to live and make it your own. Spend money on a coat of paint if the place needs it: you need a place of shelter from the storms. Living a free-lance life, as most artists do, requires that you build into your life a routine, a support group, financial security, decent food and an atmosphere that nurtures you.

If you intend to work every day from 9 to 3, do it, but also, be sure to go to the gym or walk from 7:30 to 8:30 or participate in some other activity that includes both exercise *and* regular contact with people. Fight the temptation to eat junk food. It is more convenient, but your mind and body will both pay for it later. If all you have in the house is carrots and celery, that's what you'll eat. At least make it harder on yourself to get candy and Fritos by not keeping any on hand.

If you don't have a nest egg to tide you over for a while, get some kind of job, preferably in the industry. Even if you do have enough money to survive for awhile, a job puts you in the company of other people, gives form to your life and enables you to keep your forward motion (or lack of it) in perspective: success is reached over time. Great success begins with a series of little successes starting with getting situated in town and being financially secure. You don't have to be rich, but you do have to have a job. Most of the studios, networks and conglomerate agencies have temp pools. If you can land a job there, you'll not only make money and meet people whose interests coincide with yours, but you'll begin to see how the business really works. It will make you feel better as you demystify the process and meet your future business partners.

Get Your Act Together

If you are in an impossible relationship or if you have any kind of addiction problem, deal with these things first. Show business takes even balanced people and chews them up and spits them out for breakfast unless they remain extremely focused and provide another life for themselves.

■ *When it came time for producer Bill Tennant's life to crash, it happened big. Cocaine addiction cost him his marriage, his savings and, ultimately, even shelter. The man who once owned a beautiful home replete with tennis court now lived on the street, trading even the gold inlays in his teeth for a fix.*
"I know I was my own worst enemy," he reflects. "Hollywood has always been a magnet attracting incomplete people who think that money and glamour can somehow make them complete. It can't, of course. You get consumed by it, not completed."
"Exec Comes Full Circle
After Descent into Despair"
Peter Bart
Daily Variety
February 5, 1993

Take time to get your bearings before you inflict yourself on the marketplace and vice-versa.

Build a Support Group

Life is easier with friends. Begin to build relationships with your peers. There are those who say you should build friendships with people who already have what you want. I understand the thinking, but it's not my idea of a good time. It's a lot easier to live on a shoestring and/or deal with constant rejection if your friends are doing the same thing. If your friend is already directing *Murphy Brown*, or already has her feature in pre-production and has plenty of money while you are scrambling to pay the rent, it is going to be harder to keep perspective about where you are in the process. It takes different people differing amounts of time to make the journey. Having friends who understand that will make it easier for all of you.

Attitude

One of the most valuable things you can do for yourself is to remain positive. Ruth Gordon was not only an Academy Award-winning actress (*Rosemary's Baby*) and a successful screenwriter (*Adam's Rib, Pat and Mike, etc.*), but she had an astute perspective on life:

Life is getting through the moment. The philosopher William James says to cultivate the cheerful attitude. Now nobody had more trouble than he did — except me. I had more trouble in my life than anybody. But your first big trouble can be a bonanza if you live through it. Get through the first trouble, you'll probably make it through the next one.
"The Careerist Guide to Survival"
Paul Rosenfield
The Los Angeles Times
April 25, 1982

You create your life by the choices you make in how to spend your time. You can be happy or depressed. There is no value judgment. If you choose to spend your time being depressed, which takes more energy, that's your business. It is beneficial to note that this is *your* choice. If you don't get something out of being depressed, you will take some action to change that state. It's self-indulgent to allow yourself to become more depressed.

If you are already a member of The Directors Guild or the Society of Stage Directors and Choreographers, check for support groups and/or become involved with one of their committees to help someone else. This will engage you in a productive activity with your peers on a regular basis.

Although you may be one of the lucky people who begins to work immediately, it is unlikely, so prepare yourself for a challenge, whether you are staying home or moving.

Wrap Up

Reasons to Stay Home
protected environment
it's home
cheaper to live
emotional support group in place

Home Away from Home
get a place to live with good light
establish a routine
get a job
exercise and eat well
see people every day
get involved in a support group
cultivate a positive attitude

5   Ways into the System

To enter the system successfully, you need a real
understanding of what's at stake. Hiring a director is
not like hiring an actor. If you hire an actor and he
doesn't deliver, there are other actors. You can either
replace him or you can just spend your time shooting
everything else and minimize his contribution. If the
writer doesn't come through, you know that before
you start shooting. The director must prove himself
under fire and while the meter is running:

*It's much easier to sell a beginning writer from a
script than a new director from a piece of film. A script
doesn't require the expenditure of a lot of money. If you
give someone a directing assignment, that's a whole
different thing. Even if it's a television episode, you're
turning over, in effect, a budget of several hundred
thousand dollars, or a movie for television is about
two million or a cable movie runs three million or two
and a half, so it's got to be a lot harder to get someone a
directing job.*
    Stu Robinson
    paradigm
    Los Angeles

Your success empathizing with the person who hires
you can magnify your ability to get a job. What would
you consider if you were hiring a director? What if
your money were on the line? Would you hire you?
Could you bet your most precious possession against
your ability to deliver a successful film on time and
within budget? That's what you are asking your
employer to do. If he's wrong, it's not just your career,
it could be his, too.

The Absolutely Best Way

For my money, the best way into the system is to get any kind of job working with/for a producer or director in any capacity. The list of people who started out as gofers or the equivalent with Roger Corman is impressive and endless: John Sayles, James Cameron, Amy Jones, Gale Ann Hurd are just a few.

Somebody once said that my company should be called The Corman Graduate School of Film. People know that a degree from Corman is recognized in Hollywood. Director hopefuls design projects specifically for us so that I will give them a go-ahead. The film schools do an adequate job of preparing future directors and I have occasionally given immediate assignments to film school graduates. More commonly, I hire someone for six months to two years in production and then give him or her a film to direct.

*How I Made 100 Movies in Hollywood
and Never Lost a Dime*
Roger Corman/Jim Jerome
Dell Publishing, 1991

Francis Ford Coppola is one of the lucky Corman graduates:

Roger, having heard about my theater experience and good work with actors, which was rare for a cinema type, took me on as his assistant for $90 a week. He was very proud that the winner of the Goldwyn prize was in his employ. He also made sure to tell me he once worked for $45 a week. Of course, I would have worked for him for nothing, except that I needed a meal once in a while.
    Roger was always straight—he never gave you any false hope. He was always very precise about what you

were going to get and do. It was a fabulous opportunity
for someone like me—it was better than money.

> How I Made 100 Movies in Hollywood
> and Never Lost a Dime
> Roger Corman/Jim Jerome
> Dell Publishing, 1991

When you read Roger's book, you can't help
but be inspired by the way his brain works:

*Three very successful filmmakers teamed up on
their first feature at New World when my head of
promotion, Jon Davison, bet me he could produce a film
in ten days for under $90,000. He got my trailer editors,
Allan Arkush and Joe Dante, to direct* Hollywood
Boulevard—*and won the bet. Examples like theirs still
abound. We hired a gofer recently for a four-week shoot
and by the end of the first week he had advanced to 2nd
AD. By the time we wrapped he was 1st AD, and two
pictures later I asked him to be production manager.*

> How I Made 100 Movies in Hollywood
> and Never Lost a Dime
> Roger Corman
> Dell Publishing, 1991

Corman's not the only producer who mentors
young talent. Director John Kretchmer talks about his
mentor, Steven Spielberg:

*I owe everything to Steven. I really do. He has
been enormously supportive. It was through his company
that I got my first shot at directing. No one else had given
me that opportunity.*

*I owe Steven an enormous debt just having
worked with him and having watched him work. I
watched his dedication and his caring, his unbelievable*

caring for every single frame of film. Here's a guy who has done 15 films or more and is at a point in his life where he could just coast. I have never worked with a more dedicated, more excited, enthusiastic filmmaker, ever. So often, when people get in that position, they get lazy. I'm really quite new at this.

Whenever I find myself getting down because things aren't working or I'm not given the equipment that I want, or I don't have the tools to get the performance from someone, I think of Steven and am once again reinspired to just put 110% of my effort into it. He does. He gets that from people. When people see how hard he works, it inspires them all to work at higher than we thought our capacity was.

John Kretchmer/*Director*

Linda Day, who directed the pilot and first two seasons of Married—With Children, *has given lots of people their first break. Her AD from the pilot had aspirations to direct. After a couple of seasons, she went to her producer and said, "Hey, he's ready. I'll give him one of my shots." She's helped a number of people launch their careers.*

Michael Douroux
Douroux & Co.
Los Angeles

If you just graduated from film school, working as a production assistant, doing second unit work or anything else you can do to get yourself behind the camera or assisting directors is just the next step.

Stephen Rose
Major Clients Agency
Los Angeles

A Director's Journey

Since I'm always observing people and interested in their journeys through the business, I was interested to talk to a new director who directed a segment of *Lois & Clark*. In 1975, John Kretchmer started in the business in his home town (Chicago) with the dream of being a theater producer. Although John's choice of working as a theater box office treasurer was the correct training ground, he became disillusioned, feeling that Chicago theater was not at that time as adventurous as he preferred. When a friend suggested he go to Los Angeles and explore the movie business, John was ready.

Arriving with no contacts, John checked out *Variety*'s *Films in the Future* information and contacted production offices, sending resumes to get work as a production assistant. He was waiting for a promised office job at Universal Studios to open up when his resume caught the eye of producer Jennings Lang and director Jim Goldstone who were preparing a film.

What caught their eye was not his education or his experience, but the fact that Kretchmer had gone to Amherst. Since Goldstone had attended an Ivy League school, Dartmouth, he felt a kinship. Lang and Goldstone's combined recommendation prompted Universal to call John in again and create an opportunity.

When John explained that his goal was learning how to make movies so he could produce films, Universal suggested a job in craft services. Within a week, John was on a set. For eight months he worked on a variety of films and television shows. Since John was now in the system, he surmised that the most advantageous way to learn about filmmaking (and make a decent living) would be to apply for the Assistant Director Trainee Program at the Directors Guild.

In 1977, John was admitted to the 15-month program. After graduating and working as a second assistant for two and a half years, his focus shifted from producing to directing. John knew that the absolutely fastest access for a director is good material and since he was without the financial resources to option any, John decided to take a year off and write his own. He wrote a script that was a finalist at The Sundance Institute, as well as an award-winning play that was given attention by the Williamstown Theater Festival.

Out of money, he returned to work, moving to First AD for Herbert Ross and steady work on movies. His work as Steven Spielberg's AD on *Jurassic Park* led to work on Spielberg's television show, *Seaquest,* with a proviso that he would direct. John landed two episodes of *Seaquest* and is now getting regular work directing.

His journey from his first job as the theater treasurer to directing his first show took 20 years. I asked John if, as he looked back, he could think of a choice he might have made that could have taken five years off his journey, he said he wouldn't want to:

First of all, I would not have had the opportunity to work with Steven, which really influenced me. That's an opportunity that I'm glad I didn't miss. Also, that would have been five years of working with other people who taught me things. I think I'm a better director because of those five years.

John Kretchmer/*Director*

Kenneth Frankel was Tyrone Guthrie's assistant director in the '60s at the Guthrie Theater in Minneapolis. He says that since the real training for a

director is in watching, he preferred to have something
to do while he was watching.

■ *I felt that I was better off to become a stage
manager to start with. I enjoyed doing it and it was more
important to me to know how things worked, so that
when I was directing (this still holds true), if a scenic
designer or a lighting designer comes to me and says, "We
can't do this," that I am able to say, "I think you can. I
think if you do this and this..." or if they said, "You can't
do this," to be able to find another way, as a director, to
make it work. I don't think there is any more solid way to
learn it.*
Kenneth Frankel/*Director*

■ *If I just got off the bus in New York today, my
first step would be to look into different small theater
companies, see what their programs are, try to align myself
with one and work. It's hard getting started. It's hard
getting your work seen. It shouldn't matter at all where
you direct, the idea is really about the act of directing
and working on the play. If the play is good, you won't
notice that it's in a loft someplace. As long as you can get
people to come see it, because an audience is part of
the experience.*
Jerry Zaks/*Director*

■ *There is a community of small theaters in Los
Angeles that a lot of the top directors in the business have
cut their teeth on. It's important to get involved in theater
and get agents to come see your work. It's important to
work with actors—actors are crucial to your development.
As their careers go, so can yours.*
*Being involved in the theater community doesn't
only give you a place to learn and make relationships, but
it adds credibility to your career. Every good director has*

his/her roots in theater.

When you go up to a director and say, "I know you're directing Murphy Brown, *I know you're directing* Northern Exposure, *can I observe with you?", he knows that you have been paying your dues and being of service to the community. Directors look to people who have 'done their time.'*

Stephen Rose
Major Clients Agency
Los Angeles

No Contacts?

If you are not already involved in the business in some way, other than saving Mike Ovitz from getting run over by a bus or being related to someone in the business, it will take time and persistence to work your way far enough into the system to get an agent and/or producer to meet with you or look at your reel.

Although this part of the process is extremely frustrating, the truth is that if you can't surmount this obstacle, you are in the wrong business. Show business requires so much drive and persistence that the inability to figure out how to enter the system in some way separates those who *would like to* from *those who are gonna.*

To put you into the *gonna* category, there are many possibilities.

Graduate School/They Pay You

One of the most successful ways to get into the system other than a personal recommendation is to get *any* kind of job at any studio or conglomerate talent agency.

Last year, a very qualified black female director

took a job as assistant to the executive producer of *Lois & Clark* for the express purpose of making contacts and getting inside. When the season was over, she had snagged James Earl Jones and other *L&C* guest stars to participate in her short film.

Many studios have temp pools of over-qualified people to call when an employee calls in sick. Your assignment could be anything from picking up an actor at the airport and delivering him to the set, to working in the mailroom, being a production assistant or driving a producer to appointments.

I know of several drivers who managed to gain the attention of producers who then became their advocates. Sometimes the chores may seem to be menial, but you are learning about the business hands-on within the system and getting paid for it. You can't get that in a traditional graduate school.

CineNews detailed the journey of writer/director Lark Karamardian:

Lark got hired as a temp at Fox and worked her way into her recent job as Production Coordinator of LA Law. *She was in charge of coordinating the show from the moment the script was approved—from casting to post production.*

Lark formed a partnership with another writer and they are developing projects as the Chester and Lark Company. They are about to start production on a short film that Lark has written and will direct. She plans eventually to write and direct her own plays and feature films and leave the world of television behind.

Lark Karamardian —*Writer/Director*
Michel Jones
CineNews
First Quarter — 1994

Observing

An effective way into television direction is through the practice of observing. If you know a director well enough, you might ask if he would allow you to observe. This means attending all rehearsals and tapings (and if he will allow, story conferences and note sessions) for the production of a show. A half-hour show takes five working days to produce and an hour show usually takes 7-8 working days. Movies of the Week have a much longer schedule.

You have to already be in the system in some way in order to ask this kind of a favor, but if you are motivated and persistent, who knows whom you might enlist in your behalf?

I've known several actors who wanted to make the transition to directing who began the process and gave up, for observing is a lengthy process. I also don't think they understood all the parameters of what is accomplished during the process. Agent Michael Douroux explained it very well:

There are two parts to the observation process. One is literally observing the technical process of putting together a network television show in the allotted time. The other important part is cultivating relationships. Ultimately, any director who wants to get into the main-stream of television or features is asking someone or an entity to put a tremendous amount of resources in his or her hands in order to create a viable end product. It's an enormous responsibility.

When a person is pursuing that kind of goal, if they are tenacious and they have talent and ability, they will get their shot. The essential thing is that when the shot comes, the director is in a position to make the most of it and do it in a situation where people will be supportive.

You're talking about investing as much as a year or two years of time hanging around sets observing the process while going to rehearsals and taping after taping and hanging around sets trying to build that chemistry with people who are in a position to give you a break.

Michael Douroux
Douroux & Co.
Los Angeles

There is a real distinction about observing to learn and observing with the expectation of directing a show in the future. Lee Shallat, nominated for an Emmy for her work on *Mad about You,* is now a producer-director on *The Nanny.* She got her shot because a friend recommended her to *Family Ties,* exec producer, Gary David Goldberg.

Goldberg was looking for a woman director and after five months of observing, Lee was given a show. She tries to give new directors as much help as she can, but says, unless you are an exec producer, it's pretty hard to open a door.

The key is to get in via the exec producer. I have two observers every week and a waiting list for the whole year. But they are not there on the invitation of the exec producer. I have one theater director who has been observing me for two years. He is very ready to do a show, but I cannot get him on. Few exec producers want to take risks with first-timers until the show has been running for a few years.

Lee Shallat, *Director*

Industry Temp Jobs

There are temporary agencies that specialize in providing workers for the industry in Los Angeles.

Although there is much more opportunity for this kind of job in Los Angeles, there are jobs in New York as well. You might end up working at WMA, ICM, paradigm, CAA or any of the other big agencies, production companies or networks. In New York (and even Los Angeles) there are jobs to be had with theater producing organizations like The Public, Lincoln Center, Center Theatre Group/Mark Taper Forum, etc.

You don't get to choose where you are going to work if you go through an employment agency, of course, but any destination will be illuminating.

Check the temp ads in the trades or call a studio yourself and ask if there is an in-house temporary employment pool. Many temp jobs work into regular employment if you strike the fancy of your employers and are clearly motivated. In that case, you have a chance to meet the very writers, actors and producers you're longing to work with. Obviously, you shouldn't foist yourself off on them, but you can begin relationships and, in this business, relationships are everything.

If you get a job working in the mailroom someplace, you'll have a chance to view manuscripts from hopeful writers. Perhaps you will discover someone and option the material tying yourself to the project and getting your shot.

As a director, you have to consider as many avenues towards getting your shot as possible. If you can write, that's a good way in. If you are an editor or a camera person, or have some other craft skill, that could be the way to get in. That could also be viewed as a trap, but it may not always be possible to begin a directing career by directing. If you can get an internship and observe on television and/or movies, great, but it doesn't always happen that way.

Jim Preminger
Jim Preminger Agency
Los Angeles

I'm currently a regular on *Lois & Clark*. I was surprised and pleased when one day a young director (now one of our producers) introduced himself to me and reminded me that not that many years ago, we had worked together when he was, as he described it, "a gofer or something," on a situation comedy starring Geena Davis where I played her mother. Time passes very quickly in this business.

I don't want to imply that getting an industry job is a piece of cake, but if you apply yourself, you can do it. No matter what city you live in, there is some kind of show biz community of work. Check out your local opportunities.

A word to the wise: there are daily opportunities to meet people who can help you in the business, whether you're a waiter and you become friends with a producer who comes in, or you're a driver or meet someone playing tennis. In these situations, people treat you as peers and encourage you. That's nice. Leave it there. You can allow them to know who you are and what you are doing and that you have a reel or a script. If they are interested, they will ask. If they're not and you press the issue, they can quickly become very cold toward you. Most people like to think they are discovering a new talent. If you ask, then it makes them feel as though they are being used. Allow them to discover you.

Writing as a Second Language

If you have any writing ability at all, nurture it.
Directors are unable to show their vision without
material to showcase. Part of being a good director is
knowing how material should be shaped and edited.
Many directors (to the dismay of writers) rewrite
scripts in the moment. Although there are WGA rules
against this practice, it still happens. If you are going to
do surgery on someone's creation, make sure you are
improving the material.

As I mentioned earlier, more indispensable
than a gifted director is a gifted writer-director. Two or
three manuscripts under your arm, along with your
splendid reel can spell the difference between
compliments and a job.

Take a Writer to Lunch

Director/writer relationships are natural alliances, so
for both your sakes, nurture each other. The writer
needs a director's interest as much as the director needs
access to good scripts. Robin Moran Miller was head of
the literary department at New York's prestigious
DGRW before she quit to focus more attention on
writing and to teach master scriptwriting classes. She
thinks the most logical alliance for a writer (other than
with a bankable name actor) is with a director.

*A lot of my friends who are screenwriters got their
foot in the door through a specific director that they may
have met at some school or along the line, who has liked a
script of theirs. When the director got development money,
he said, "I want to do this script."*
Robin Moran Miller
New York

■ *Good writing is the key to good directing. If the concern is displaying yourself to the best of your ability, try to find a good playwright.*
    Jerry Zaks/*Director*

■ *When a director who is also a writer goes in for a job on a film that needs work, that director can be articulate about exactly what that film needs. Being a writer is an enormous help. That plus tenacity and enthusiasm—all of those things help him get the job. Everybody wants to be in business with a good writer-director.*
    Michael Douroux
    Douroux & Co.
    Los Angeles

Agent Barry Douglas (DGRW in New York) thinks directors should always be looking for talented playwrights. He thinks the chances of being hired for regional work around the country are enhanced because the director can then pitch a package. He can say: "I have this excellent new play that I want to direct. I know this playwright and we have a relationship." Along with showing his reviews, he thinks this is the perfect entree.

Jonathan Tolins

It was my pleasure to attend the opening of a play written by Jonathan Tolins at The Pasadena Playhouse. I met Jon when he stage-managed a play at The Matrix Theater in Los Angeles. A year later, he wrote, produced and directed his own first play. His second play, *Twilight of the Golds* went to Broadway via The Kennedy Center and has been sold as a film. Tolins' focus is writing and acting, but the brilliance with which he tracked his career is inspiring.

When he was only four years out of college, his name was all over the trades. Here's a guy who is not only talented and motivated, but very, very smart:

■ *Even at 26, Tolins clearly knows the business. His* Twilight *script was rejected for a reading at one theater, he concedes, but he also turned down possible productions in small local houses. He put up $500 of his own money for a reading of* Twilight *last July to widen his producer net: "I really felt I had something that might have commercial potential."*
"Tales from the Front"
Barbara Isenberg
The Los Angeles Times
February 14, 1993

Tolins graduated from Harvard in 1988 with an impressive theatrical university resume. A triple threat, Jon had acted, directed and won a major literary award. Upon arriving in LA, he got a job writing questions for a game show. He says he wrote *Twilight* while temping at studios. Jon managed to do all the things the agents tell you to do: produce your own work, be visible and work in the industry.

Another way into a connected environment is to get into an acting or writing class either as a participant or an auditor. As you join in the collaboration and experience first hand the problems of actors and writers, you will be better at working with both.

■ *Go to a lot of theater, meet a lot of people and when you meet a writer whose work you really like, contact him personally, because writers are always looking for directors.*
Robin Moran Miller
New York

Play Festivals

Play festivals are a double whammy for directors. You can meet important agents and producers while you are all scouting the new great American playwright. And if you are directing these new geniuses, no one will miss your contribution.

The best source of information for play festivals (as well as names of theaters, their administrators, addresses and phone numbers) is *The Dramatists Sourcebook*. The book is crammed with information of every type. It's slanted for playwrights, of course, but since you have some of the same needs that they do, it's a *must have* for your reference shelf.

The Dramatist Sourcebook is published by Theater Communications Group, who also publish *Theater Directory*, an annual directory providing complete contact information on more than 300 nonprofit professional theaters and over 40 arts resource organizations.

Theater Communications Group
355 Lexington Avenue
New York, NY 10017

Film and Video Festivals

The value of exposing your material at the right festival cannot be overstated. In 1989, an unknown director arrived at the Sundance Film Festival gripping a can of film and praying for a miracle. The attention gained by a rave review in *Variety* and winning the Dramatic Competition Audience Award for his film, *sex, lies, and videotape,* changed Steven Soderberg's life.

The breadth of the festival circuit is astounding with competitions as diverse as those sponsored by the

Academy of Motion Picture Arts and Sciences for a variety of filmmakers (students, short films, documentaries, animated films, etc.) to Sundance, Cannes, The New York Lesbian and Gay Experimental Film Festival, the International Wildlife Film Festival and on and on. Some festivals require entry fees of $375 (International Film and TV Festival of New York) and some, like Cannes, are free. Although some prizes include money (many are only awards), the real value is in having your film seen by the film community.

Just being invited to a festival, however, is not enough. The trick is to gain admittance to the right festival,

Deciding what festival to enter is one of the most important promotional decisions an indie producer can make. In North America, the crucial fests are those that grant access to the National. Toronto, Sundance, New York and even Telluride are the most noteworthy.

From an acquisitions standpoint, Cannes and Toronto are considered to be the strongest overall. Though for strictly American product, Sundance is preeminent. (Many producers hold their films back from other fests in order to premiere at Sundance). New York and Telluride are generally thought to be weaker festivals for acquisitions. More European buyers and festival directors are also coming to Toronto and Sundance these days.

For European independents, Cannes and Berlin are best for snagging global distribution, while Venice is strong regionally for Italian distribution. Smaller festivals such as those in Rotterdam, Locarno, Thessalonika and San Sebastian are also getting closer looks by European as

well as American buyers.
"Which Fest is Best?"
James Ulmer
The Hollywood Reporter 1994
Independent Producers & Distributors Special Issue

If this route interests you, you must own *The AIFV Guide for International Film and Video Festivals* by Kathryn Bowser. The book is published by the Foundation for Independent Video and Film, Inc. and lists specifics for hundreds of national and international film and video festivals and, for some, a narrative of a specific year's events.

The foundation is the affiliate of the Association of Independent Video and Filmmakers (AIVF) and supports a variety of programs and services for the independent media community.

FIVF
625 Broadway, 9th Floor
New York, NY 10012
212-473-3400/fax 212-677-8732
aivffivf@aol.com

A Few Competitions

Academy Awards/Documentary Film Competition
Academy of Motion Picture Arts and Sciences
8949 Wilshire Blvd.
Beverly Hills, CA 90211-1972
310-278-8990/fax 310-859-9351
Formats: 35 mm, 16 mm
Entry fee: None
Month held: Early December
Deadline: Late October
Category: Documentary/Award
Contact: AMPAS Director

Cannes International Film Festival
71, rue du Faubourg St. Honore
75008 Paris, France
1 42 66 92 20/fax 1 42 66 68 85/tlx FESTIFI 650 765 F
Formats: 35 mm, 16 mm
Entry fee: None
Month held: Mid-May
Deadline: Mid-March
Category: General/Market
Contact: Gilles Jacob, General Delegate

Sundance Film Festival
3619 Motor Avenue
Los Angeles, CA 90034
801-204-2091/fax 801-645-7280
Formats: 35 mm, 16 mm, preview on ¾" or ½"

The above festival information was gleaned from the
AIVF Guide with their permission.

The listings in the AIVF Guide are much more
comprehensive and are quite extensive. They list by
geography, deadline and category. They also include
information regarding shipping and useful international country codes. I got my book at Samuel French
Bookstore in Los Angeles for $29.95. I'm sure any film
library would have a copy.

Independent Film Channel

Another avenue for your independent film is the new
Independent Film Channel. The advisory board includes Robert Altman, Spike Lee, Martin Scorsese and
other directors you'd like to have in your corner.

    Dedicated entirely to independent films and

---

programs about their creation, IFC will be distributed
by Bravo Cable Network....Over the next year, the
channel will provide financing for 8 to 12 short films by
emerging filmmakers.

Interest in student filmmaking has grown with
the popularity of independent films and the channel will
sponsor a university showcase at the annual Independent
Film Market in mid-September at the Angelika Film
Center in Manhattan. Work from eight film schools will
be chosen for screening at the market: Boston University;
Columbia University; New York University; San
Francisco State University; the School of Visual Arts; the
University of California at Los Angeles; the University of
Southern California and the University of Texas at
Austin. One of the eight films will receive the Bravo/IFC
Outstanding Student Film of 1994 Award, which includes
a cash prize of $10,000 and the opportunity to make a
short film for Bravo/IFC.

"Making Films Before Fame Knocks"
Jennifer Dunning
The New York Times
September 1, 1994

Does Studying Help?

Although this book is intended for directors who have
already studied (if they're going to), there may be some
readers who are not that far along with their directing
or who, though having directed, still think studying
might enhance their chances. I've collected a few
opinions as well as information on the connected
places to study.

During an event at The Directors Guild, Barry
Levinson, Oliver Stone and Barbra Streisand discussed
the art of filmmaking and study:

Asked about the foundations of their art and craft, all admitted to feeling that their directorial skills and careers owed more to love of the creative process and trust in the creative instinct than to any specific type of education. As Levinson put it, "I'm not sure how you learn to do what we do—or, in fact, how you do what we do."

"Directors on Directing"
Joel Deutsch
DGA News
April–May 1992

I don't know how anybody can really define themselves as a director for movies or television if they do not have certain technical fundamentals down. I don't know where you get those fundamentals. I suppose it would be in film school or interning. I know there are people who have, in effect, become film directors because they just said they were, but I don't really know how that comes about. There are people like Oliver Stone who seem to appear, but he had been in Hollywood in the film business for a long time. There is something called osmosis that takes over.

Gary Salt
Paul Kohner, Inc.
Los Angeles

I guess classes can't hurt. I wouldn't say, "This is how you are going to be a success, go to class." I've had successes with people who are AFI graduates and from UCLA and USC film school and I've had success with people who were plumbers and bus drivers and whatever. I would say, generally, that college-educated people have a higher percentage of scores.

Stu Robinson
paradigm
Los Angeles

■ *Yale and NYU are not the only places for theater
directors to attract some attention; Pittsburgh and North
Carolina have both made a big difference in the industry.*
Barry Douglas
DGRW
New York

Kenneth Frankel, who was a staff director at
both Long Wharf (Connecticut) and the Guthrie
Theater (Minnesota) says the most important training
for a theater director is to go to an undergraduate
school that *doesn't* have a professional theater program:

■ *You don't need a professional training program
as a director. What you need to do is spend time learning
everything in the world—all about art, all about history,
all about clothing, all about politics—everything. You
need to be able to watch a lot of stuff.*
Kenneth Frankel/*Director*

Whether or not the schools are helpful may be second-
ary to the possibility of getting accepted:

■ *NYU— In 1987 there were 497 applicants. In 1992
there were 890 applicants. The number admitted in each of
those years was 52. USC—In 1988 there were 583
applicants. In 1992, there were 864. In 1988, they admitted
110. In 1992, the number was 188. Graduates of USC's
School of Cinema have received 30 Academy Awards.*
The Guinness Book of
Movie Facts and Feats
Patrick Robertson
Guinness Publishing
Great Britain

Film Schools That Can Make a Difference

Even if film and theater schools merely provide a laboratory and mentors, some do it in a first class way:

■ *NYU, USC and UCLA can marshal enormous resources compared to lesser known schools. They have much more equipment than even state run studios in developing countries. They are centrally organized, with large administrative staffs including development directors, public relations consultants, and numerous support staff. USC actually has a director of student-industry relations who, for all intents and purposes, functions as an agent for students.*

Located in the vortex of the two most important production centers in the U. S.—New York and Los Angeles—these programs engage in symbiosis with the industry, borrowing professionals as adjuncts, hosting preview screeenings and regularly bringing in guests.

Patricia R. Zimmermann
The Independent Film & Video Monthly
August/September 1994

This information from *The New York Times* chronicles a few of the better known film schools:

■ *American Film Institute, Center for Advanced Film and Television Studios, Los Angeles. Non-degree program.*

Number of students: In the first year about 140, of whom 70 are asked back for a second year.

Films made per year: 84 short films in the first year, 8 in the second. Students work in teams.

Famous alumni: Martin Brest, Carl Franklin, Amy Heckerling, Marshall Herskovitz, David Lynch, Terrence Malik, Edward Zwick.

■ *Columbia University School of the Arts, Film Division, New York.*
Number of students: About 240 students in the graduate program, 35 in the undergraduate program.
Films made per year: About 50 short films in the graduate program.
Famous alumni: Katherine Bigelow, Stacy Cochran.

■ *New York University, Tisch School of the Arts, Institute of Film and Television*
Number of students: 1,050 undergraduates, 150 graduate students.
Films made per year: About 4,000, with many students making two or three short films or one feature film.
Famous alumni: Joel Coen, Chris Columbus, Martha Coolidge, Ernest Dickerson, Jim Jarmusch, Martin Brest, Amy Heckerling, Spike Lee, Martin Scorcese, Oliver Stone, Susan Seidelman.

■ *University of Southern California, School of Cinema-Television, Los Angeles.*
Number of students: 277 graduate students, 195 undergraduate students.
Films made per year: About 2,000, 45 of which are senior-level thesis projects.
Famous alumni: John Carpenter, Ron Howard, Brian Glaser, James Ivory, Phil Joanou, Randal Kleiser, George Lucas, Paul Mazursky, John Milius, John Singleton, Robert Zemeckis.

■ *University of California at Los Angeles, School of Theater, Film and Television*
Number of students: 255 in the film and television graduate program, 63 in the undergraduate

program.

Films made per year: 80 to 100, including videos.

Famous alumni: Francis Ford Coppola, Colin Higgins, Neil Jimenez, Tim Robbins, Penelope Spheeris, Paul Bartel, David S. Ward.

"School Days for Future Stars"
William Grimes
The New York Times
January 17, 1993

Agents think highly of USC and answer phone calls from any UCLA or AFI teacher who recommends a promising student. The proximity of these schools to the world's movie capital ensures participation of the famous screenwriters, producers and directors as guest speakers and guest teachers in the extension program.

Other Contenders

Even if you are lucky enough to gain admittance to one of these schools, you could get lost in the geniuses. An instructive article in *The Independent*, a publication of the Foundation for Independent Video and Film makes a cogent case for taking another tack:

▰ *Film departments no longer obsess over proficiency in the operation of Arriflex cameras and Moviolas. Many faculty members debunk the myth of film school as a training ground for entry level jobs. In a major shift from the seventies, professors and administrators at a wide variety of schools emphasize liberal arts as the academic bedrock of filmmaking. One professor declared, "We are in the business of granting college degrees that have some larger meaning, not serving as employment*

---

agencies for multinational corporations."

...Graduates of the 'big three' do bear a certain cachet in the industry, have access to high-profile internships and benefit from niceties like special screenings of student work for industry executives. Their classrooms are filled with an endless stream of industry guests almost unimaginable in other educational contexts. These film schools also have many more students than most of the programs described here: 1,000 undergrads at NYU compared to 20 at Iowa.

"Film Schools Not To Be Overlooked"
Patricia R. Zimmermann
The Independent Film & Video Monthly
August/September 1994

The excellent article focused on many superior film schools that represent diversity and demonstrate a commitment to independent film that Zimmerman feels far surpasses the more illustrious schools:

Films schools on the periphery are the incubators of independent filmmaking, often defining themselves as outposts of regional cinema. Rather than producing workers for the industry, these schools see themselves as educating active producers who will make choices outside of commercial norms and give voice to those on the margins.

"Film Schools Not To Be Overlooked"
Patricia R. Zimmermann
The Independent Film & Video Monthly
August/September 1994

Zimmerman went on to list nine other recommended film schools. The article is too long to quote, but I will mention the film schools and some pertinent information,

---

Temple University—Philadelphia, Pennsylvania.
Enrollment undergrad: 1,000/grad 70-80. Undergrad
tuition: $5,000 PA residents/$7,000 grad out-of-state.
Prominent faculty includes Julie Gustafson, Eran Preis,
Warren Bass, David Parry, Peter d'Agostino, Alan
Powell, Jeff Rush. Alumni: Lise Yasue, Wendy
Weinberg, Thomas Ott, Jan Krawitz, Radha Barwajaz,
Nina Gilberty.

Ohio University—Athens, Ohio. Enrollment:
undergrad: 50-60 (minor)/9 honors tutorial/grad: 45.
Tuition: $3,000 OH residents/$6,700 out-of-state.
Prominent faculty includes Rajko Grlic, Ruth Bradley.
Alumni: Tony Buba, Ed Lachman, Eran Preis, Steve
Hank.

Montana State University—Bozeman, Montana.
Enrollment undergrad: 200-215. Tuition: $5,000 MT
residents/$6,000 out-of-state. Prominent faculty
includes Dennis Alg, Ronald Tobias, Dan Hart, Paul
Monaco. Alumni: Ed Jones, Mark Vargo.

Emerson College—Boston, Massachusetts. Enrollment:
undergrad 350. Tuition: $24,000. Prominent faculty
includes Bridget Murname, Claire Andrade-Watkins,
Patty Romeo, Jane Shattuc. Alumni: Spalding Gray,
Vincent DiBona, Norman Lear.

University of Iowa—Iowa City, Iowa. Enrollment
undergrad, 220/grad 12. Tuition: $1,145 IO residents/
out-of-state. Grad $1,360 IO residents/$4,246 out-of-
state. Prominent faculty includes Franklin Miller,
Leighton Pierce, J. Dudley Andrew, Lauren
Rabinowitz. Alumni: Mark Johnson, Tom Ackerman,
Bob Seaman, Bob Watzke.

University of Wisconsin/Milwaukee—Milwaukee, Wisconsin. Enrollment: undergrad: 100 grad/10 (12 limit). Tuition: undergrad $1,273 WI residents/ $4,075 out-of-state; grad. $1,764 WI residents/$5,299 out-of-state. Prominent faculty includes Cecelia Condt, Portia Cobb, Diane Kitchen, Rob Danielson. Alumni: Cathy Cook, Chris Bratton.

University of Texas/Austin—Enrollment: undergrad 100/grad 10-12. Tuition: undergrad $713/grad $798 TX residents $2,345/grad $1,968 out-of-state. Prominent faculty include Robert Foshka, Nicholos Sominos, Janet Staiger. Alumni: Michael Zinberg, Jordan Levin, Wayne Lemon, Bernard Lechowick, Bob Levy, Robert Rodriguez, Julie Cypher.

Wright State—Dayton, Ohio. Enrollment: 95. Tuition: $3,000. Prominent faculty includes James Klein, Julia Reichert, Russ Johnson, Chuck Derry, Bill Lafferty.

Ithaca College—Ithaca, New York. Enrollment 130 in BS 150 in BFA. Tuition: $14,000. Prominent faculty includes: Michael Nathanson, Daniel Heffner, Jonathan Heap, Mark Romanek, Judy Marks, Rapiered Thompson. Alumni: Michael Nathanson, Daniel Heffner, Jonathan Heap, Mark Romanek, Judy Marks.

The above was condensed from an article in *The Independent Film & Video* by Patricia R. Zimmerman in the August/September 1994 issue.

Theater Schools

Prestigious schools that train directors include:

American Repertory Theater
Robert Brustein, Artistic Director
Harvard University/Loeb Drama Department
64 Brattle Street
Cambridge, Massachusetts 02138
(617) 495-2668

Boston University/Theater Arts Division
Robert Croucher
855 Commonwealth Avenue
Boston, Massachusetts 02215
(617) 353-3390

Carnegie Mellon/Drama Department
Elisabeth Orion
5000 Forbes Avenue
Pittsburgh, Pennsylvania 15213
(412) 268-2082

Catholic University/Department of Drama
Dr. Gitta Honegger
620 Michigan Avenue NE
Washington, District of Columbia 20064
(202) 319-5358

Juilliard School
Michael Kahn
60 Lincoln Center Plaza
New York City, New York 10023
(212) 799-5000, Ext. 4

New York University/Theater Department
Arthur Barstow, Chairperson
721 Broadway 3rd floor (at Waverly Place)
New York City, New York 10003
(212) 998-1850

North Carolina School of the Arts
Department of Drama/Gerald Freeman
200 Waughtown Street
Winston-Salem, North Carolina 27717-2189
(910) 770-3399

Southern Methodist University
Department of Playwrighting and Directing
P. O. Box 286
Dallas, Texas 75275
(214) 768-2558

State University of New York (at Purchase)
Theater Department
Israel Hicks
735 Anderson Hill Road
Purchase, New York 10577
(914) 251-6000

University of California (at San Diego)
Department of Theater/Directors Program
Andrei Belgrade
9300 Gelman Drive
La Jolla, California 92093-0344
(619) 534-6889

Yale School of Drama/Stan Wojewodski, Jr.
P. O. Box 208244
New Haven, Connecticut 06520
(203) 432-1505

Florence Stanley is best known as a successful Broadway, film and television actress, but she has also directed for theater and television. I asked if she were going to study directing, which school she would pick:

■   *If I were going to study directing, I would take a basic course in directing at any school. I would not expect to learn much except from the textbook. I would proceed to try to get a variety of directors to let me observe from beginning to end. Especially directors whose work I liked.*
  Florence Stanley/Actress-Director

Other Kinds of Study

Whether or not film school is the answer, there are other avenues of study that can not only inform your directing, but change your life. In Roger Corman's autobiography, he discusses acting classes:

■   *That shoot left me thinking that if I really wanted to improve as a director, I would have to learn more about actors and their process. And so, immediately after* Sorority Girl, *I enrolled in classes with the great acting coach, Jeff Corey. I had asked Jeff if I could just come in and observe. Jeff didn't go along with the concept of observing and welcomed me only if I participated. He was quite correct. I met and worked with some fine talents. I first met Jack Nicholson there and I would soon be using Jack in some of my films. I also met Robert Towne, before his screenwriter/director days. I went to weekly classes for a couple of years and the class proved to be invaluable training for me.*
  How I Made a Hundred Movies In
  Hollywood and Never Lost a Dime
  Roger Corman/Jim Jerome
  Dell Publishing, 1991

Support Groups

Whether you are in a support group allied with your film class at a connected institution or have pulled together your own collective, support groups not only provide comfort and a place to blow off steam, but are conduits of information and access. Some groups are more tied in to what is going on than others, but whenever you enlist others on the same journey, you broaden your perspective.

In terms of coping as a director, being connected to a group is crucial. Because a director's resources are the play and the actors, there's nothing more critical than being involved. Being connected to a home is crucial. It's critical that you work on material that excites you. Try to find a playwright (hopefully living) whose work you love and become a team.

Jerry Zaks/*Director*

Association of Independent Video and Film, Inc..

The largest membership association of independent film and video makers in the country, AIVF, provides a broad range of services and resources for the field, including health and production insurance, trade discounts, networking opportunities, advocacy referrals and access to the publications and programs offered by AIVF's affiliate, the Foundation for Independent Video and Film (FIVF). Membership ranges from $25/student to $150/industry: individual membership is $45 and includes a subscription to the monthly magazine, *The Independent*.

AIVF
625 Broadway, 9th Floor
New York, NY 10012
212-677-8732
aivffivf@aol.com

AWE

The Association of Women in Entertainment is a small support group organized to promote the advancement of women in the Entertainment Industry through networking, job referral and education. The only requirement for membership is the desire to support women in the entertainment industry. Dues are $50 for one year. AWE meets the fourth Monday of the month at 7:15 p.m. at The Dino Laurentiis Building, 8670 Wilshire Blvd., Beverly Hills.

The Association of Women in Entertainment
PO Box 93792
Los Angeles, CA 90093-0792
213-896-8242

Chanticleer Films/The Discovery Program

The Discovery Program is a program for beginning directors. It is specifically designed to give working professionals in the entertainment industry an opportunity to direct a short film. If you are already in the business in any position, you are eligible for consideration for this program. The Program is designed to offer directing opportunities to those who need it most. Therefore, prior directorial experience must be very limited. Write for particulars. If you are chosen, Chanticleer will furnish up to $60,000, some production services and the chance to have your work shown to at least one major studio.

Chanticleer Films
1680 Vine Street, Suite 1212
Hollywood, CA 90028
213-462-4705

Cinewomen

Cinewomen is a non-partisan, non-profit organization
of professional women in the entertainment industry,
whose purpose is supporting the advancement of
women and their career goals in a non-competitive
environment. Dedicated to developing the number and
range of opportunities available to women in the
industry, this group seems to be effective in stimulating
its members to put their material out there. They
publish a quarterly newsletter, *CineNews*.

Cinewomen
9903 Santa Monica Boulevard #461
Beverly Hills, CA 90212
310-855-8720

Independent Features Projects

One of the most connected and effective support
groups for filmmakers is IFP. Their 6000-plus members
across the country include directors, grips, writers,
sound technicians and anyone involved or wanting to
be involved in independent film. This non-profit group
produces seminars, classes, screenings, producer series,
The Spirit Awards and an eclectic collection of
industry-related resources.

It is not necessary to be a member in order to
attend events, but the regular newsletter is only
available to members. It is full of information regarding free screenings, get togethers, resource listings for
equipment, independent financing sources, a discount
vendor list and membership career news. Membership
is $50 for students, $85 for individuals with higher fees
for corporate sponsorships.

IFP 212-465-8200
IFP West Los Angeles 310-392-8832
IFP Midwest 312-736-7009
IFP North Minneapolis 612-338-0871
IFP South Miami 305-672-9297

The Stage Directors and Choreographers Foundation

This foundation allied with The Society of Stage
Directors and Choreographers is the only organization
in the country providing services primarily for stage
directors and choreographers. Established in 1965,
SD&CF sponsors workshop productions, regional
seminars, roundtables, resource publications, a library
and a monthly newsletter, *SSDC Notes.*

SSDC Foundation
1501 Broadway, Suite 2003
New York, NY 10036
212-302-5359/fax 212-302-6195

New Dramatists

New Dramatists is dedicated to finding gifted playwrights and giving them the time, space and tools to
develop their craft so that they may fulfill their potential and make lasting contributions to the theater.

If you become involved with this group, either
by attending their readings or volunteering to direct a
project, you will not only enhance your chances to
direct, but you may find your own private playwright.

New Dramatists
424 W 44th Street
New York, NY 10036
212-757-6960

International Information

The International Theater Institute—is an organization started in 1948 by UNESCO committed to fostering theater communication with 82 centers around the world. Not only a conduit for information, ITI provides entree for artists of all kinds (actors, writers, directors, etc.), who are either going abroad or considering it. ITI puts out a quarterly newsletter that's yours for a contribution and maintains an extensive research library that is available to anyone doing serious research:

The International Theater Institute
ITI of the United States
Louis A. Rachow
220 W 42nd Street #1710
New York, NY 10035

ITI director, Louis Rachow turned me on to other sourcebooks that are available at ITI or from the institutions listed:

The Original British Theater Directory

Richmond House Publishing Co. Ltd.
9-11 Richmond Buildings London IV5AF
telephone 44-071-437-9556/telefax 44-071-434-0200

The British Alternative Theater Directory

Rebecca Books
Ivor House, Suite #2
1 Bridge Street
Cardiff CF12TH Wales
telephone 44-022-237-8452/telefax 344 022-223-8690

The Performing Arts Yearbook for Europe

Arts Publishing International, Ltd.
4 Assam St.
London E17QS
telephone 44-071-247-0066telefax 44-071-247-6868

Price listed on the cover is in pounds sterling with no US equivalent, but Louis says PAYE (Performing Arts Yearbook for Europe) costs about $50.00 and the other books listed are about $30.00 each.

The Dramatists Sourcebook

Although *The Dramatists Sourcebook* is a book dedicated to scriptwriter information, since their extensive list of grants, scholarships, contests and prizes for scriptwriters lists the names and address of venues where both actors and directors are available to give support, this seems like a perfect resource for directors looking to hook up with peers to produce material. The book is available in bookstores as well as from:

Theater Communications Group
355 Lexington Avenue
New York, NY 10017
212-697-5230

Be Informed

It is imperative to understand who your buyers are and recognize the current trends. If action is in and you're known for your comedic style, you'll realize the rejection is not personal. You're just not where the business is right now. The pendulum will be coming your way again in the future. For film and television directors, I recommend that you subscribe to one or both of the daily Los Angeles trades, as well as the monthly magazine of the Directors Guild.

Theater Week is a valuable source of national theater news. A subscription is $29.95 for 12 issues.

Daily Variety 5700 Wilshire Blvd. Los Angeles, CA 90036 213-857-6600	*The Hollywood Reporter* 5055 Wilshire Blvd. Los Angeles, CA 90036 213-525-2000
The DGA News 7920 Sunset Boulevard Los Angeles, CA 90046 310-289-2034/5	
Theater Week 28 W 25th Street, 4th Floor New York, NY 10010 212-627-2120	

Daily Variety sells for $1.00 a copy and *The Hollywood Reporter* costs $1.50 a copy. *The DGA News* is indispensable for staying plugged into the film and television scene. Published bi-monthly, it costs $4.50 per single issue. A one-year subscription is $25.00 (US) and $35.00 (foreign).

Read Everything

An article in *The New York Times* regarding the then 33-year-old writer-director Stacy Cochran (*My New Gun*) was instructive not only on the career smart-moves of Ms. Cochran, but peripherally gave information about the wants and needs of Los Angeles-based IRS Media which recently brought out *One False Move* and *Gas Food and Lodging*:

■ My New Gun *was budgeted at $2.1 million with financing from IRS Media and Columbia TriStar Home Video. According to Paul Colichman, an executive producer at IRS, the company is interested in movies by first-time directors that have a strong sense of style. The company also looks for films that might attract art house, video and pay-per-view television audiences.*

"*My New Gun* Hits Its Makers' Target"
Marsha McCreadie
The New York Times
October 25, 1992

Your Reference Library

Books that have the credits of writers, directors, actors, casting directors and producers should be part of your reference collection. In addition to whatever books on directing that you own, I strongly suggest you begin assembling a library stocked with books that give you an idea of what the business is really like. It's not that the business is so bad, but it is tough. Biographies of successful people will provide role models in your quest for achievement and may even inform your goals. Big success requires big sacrifices. Don't find out later that the cost was too high. Denial is said to be even more potent than cocaine; neither drug enhances your marketability.

Here is a list of books that will give your library a good start:

Academy Players Directory/Academy of Motion
       Picture Arts and Sciences
Adventures in the Screen Trade/William Goldman
*AIVF Guide to International Film
       and Video Festivals*/Kathryn Bowser
Art of War/Sun Tzu edited by James Clavell

*casting by.../*A Directory of the Casting Society of
America, its members and their credits
*Complete Directory to Primetime Network
TV Shows/*Tim Brooks-Earle Marsh
*Creating Unforgettable Characters/*Linda Seger
*Directing the Action/*Charles Marowitz
*The Devil's Candy/*Julie Salamon
*Dramatists Sourcebook/*Theater
Communications Group
*The Directors Guild of America Directory of Members
Film Finance & Distribution: a Dictionary of
Terms/*John W. Cones
*The Film Encyclopedia/*Ephraim Katz
*The Filmgoer's Companion/*Leslie Halliwell
*Film Producers, Studios, Agents, Casting Directors
Guide/*David M. Kipen & Jack Lechner
*Final Cut/*Steven Bach
*Halliwell's Film Guide/*Leslie Halliwell
*Hollywood Agents Directory/*Hollywood
Creative Directory
*Hollywood on $5,000, $10,000, or $25,000
a Day/*Philip Gaines & David Rhodes
*How I Made a Hundred Movies in Hollywood and Never
Lost a Dime/*Roger Corman
*Hype & Glory/*William Goldman
*Indecent Exposure/*David McClintock
*The Last Great Ride/*Brandon Tartikoff
*Making a Good Script Great/*Linda Seger
*Method or Madness/*Bobby Lewis
*NY Times Directory of Film/*Arno Press
*NY Times Directory of Theater/*Arno Press
*Playwright's Companion/*Feedback Theater Books
*Reel Power/*Mark Litwak
*Saturday Night Live/*Doug Hall/Jeff Weingrad
Screen World current edition/*John Willis
*Screenwriter's Workbook/*Syd Field

Screenwriting Tricks of the Trade/William Froug
The Season/William Goldman
Theater World current edition/John Willis
TV Movies/Leonard Maltin
What a Producer Does/Buck Houghton
Who's Who in American Film Now/James Monaco
Who's Who in Television/Rodman Gregg
Who's Who in the Motion Picture
        Industry/Rodman Gregg
Wired/Bob Woodward
The Writers Guild of America Membership Directory
You'll Never Eat Lunch in This
        Town Again/Julia Phillips

The *Who's Who* books by Rodman Gregg
(Packard House Books, Beverly Hills, CA) and the
*Film Producers, Studios, Agents and Casting Directors
Guide* by David M. Kipen and Jack Lechner (Lone
Eagle Publishing Company, Los Angeles) are
particularly helpful; they list directors, producers,
producing companies, their credits and contact
addresses.

The Academy Players Directory, published by
The Academy of Motion Picture Arts and Sciences, is
an indispensable reference tool for tracking actors. The
APD costs $65. Back issues are sold at a fraction of the
original price.

I particularly recommend *What a Producer
Does*. Three chapters specifically bear reading: those
dealing with the hiring of directors, actors and writers.

Charles Marowitz's book about directing for
the theater also sets forth valuable information about
actors and casting. Roger Corman's book is a must for
anyone involved with the business. It's entertaining
and inspirational.

The DGA, WGA and SSDC membership
directories are helpful for tracking people's agents and

credits and generally keeping abreast of your peers. They are free to members, but are available for a fee to non-members through the guilds.

Directors Guild of America West 7920 Sunset Blvd. Los Angeles, CA 90046 310-289-2000	Directors Guild of America 520 N Michigan Ave. Chicago, IL 60611 312-644-5050
Directors Guild of America 110 W 57th St. New York, NY 10019 212-581-0370	Directors Guild of Great Britain 56 Whitfield Street London Wl England 71-880-9582
Writers Guild/West 8955 Beverly Blvd. W Hollywood, CA 90048 310-550-1000	Writers Guild/East 555 West 57th St. New York, NY 10019 212-767-7800
Society of Stage Directors & Choreographers P. O. Box 93847 Hollywood, CA 90093 310-854-6656	
Society of Stage Directors & Choreographers 1501 Broadway, 31st floor New York, NY 10036 212-391-1070/fax 212-302-6195	

Whether or not directing a movie is the equivalent of engaging in war, many who aspire to showbiz stardom find *The Art of War* indispensable. This quote illustrates one of the reasons why:

If you know the enemy and know yourself, you need not fear the result of a hundred battles. If you know yourself but not the enemy, for every victory gained you will also suffer a defeat. If you know neither the enemy nor yourself, you will succumb in every battle.

> The Art of War
> Sun Tzu
> Edited by James Clavell
> Delta Press, 1988

Wrap Up

Ways Into the System
industry job
writing workshops
acting classes
directing classes
study at industry connected institutions

Film Support
Independent Features Project
The Discovery Program

Theater Support
Playwrights Horizons
The Public Theater
Ensemble Studio Theater
The New Dramatists

Keep Informed
reference library
read the trades
DGA membership listings
WGA membership listings
SSDC Directory of Members

6   Agents, Finally

You've been very patient. I know you have been dying to jump to this part of the book from the moment you bought it because getting an agent takes on enormous significance in the quest for credibility. Not being able to get an agent hurts feelings, makes people hostile and undermines self confidence.

Whether by choice or circumstances, a good number of directors listed in the DGA membership directory don't have agents. Most name directors do have agents and those who don't frequently list managers or attorneys.

In most cases, a good agent can certainly enhance your career. But unless you are already making money, it's difficult to get an agent to talk to you, take a meeting or in any other way validate your existence. Some feel you can make an entire career out of getting an agent.

Even though the quest for an agent can become a full time job in itself, untried people still manage to get agents and enter the business hourly. These new people are often related to others in the business or otherwise connected, giving them entree. Most, however are driven, clever, ingenious and of course, very talented. Many are all of the above.

How the Business Really Works

Over the course of my career as both an actress and an author, I have met many *wanna-bes*. I distinguish the *wannas* from the *gonnas* because the WBs all think someone else is to blame for their problems: "So and so doesn't like me" or "Well, I'm not related to anyone in the business, so I'll never make it" or "If I can just get invited to that party" or "play tennis with so and so" or "sleep with so and so." By contrast, GBs say: "What? There's no door here? I'll build one."

Nepotism exists in any business, but as in any other business, it only exists until it begins to cost people money. Particularly at the directing level, there is too much money at stake to hand unqualified people the reins. If you demonstrate that you know what you are doing, have a personal style that creates a commercial product and that you can take responsibility, you will get your shot. You may have to finance it yourself to start with, but you will get your chance.

This book exists for all of you without obvious entree who have made the commitment to succeed. I have researched the marketplace investigating ways to make the paths from the outside to the inside and from the inside to further in a little easier. I talked to film and theater directors, agents and producers. I haunted bookstores trying to find any book that I thought might be helpful in building a career philosophy as well as mentor the solitary life of the director. You must know everything and you can lose face if you confide to anyone that you're stymied or don't know how to do something. It can be lonely.

Since agents are as interested as you are in your success, I asked their advice. Their quotes are gleaned from interviews with scores of agents in Los Angeles and New York, who represent directors for the theater, film, and television. The agents reveal their ideas on how neophyte directors might enter the marketplace, help themselves, attract agents and move toward their career goals in the most timely and intelligent manner.

Why Agents?

Agents exist because there is a need. The buyers could not possibly cull through all the reels, query letters, screenings and phone calls vying for their attention without some kind of screening process. I know right now it doesn't seem like such a bad idea that they should look at everything that comes in (your reel or resume, for instance), but believe me, once you are in the system, you will not want your agent taking time away from your career to scout your competiton.

Do I Need One?

Not all directors have agents. Because of the entrepreneurial skills needed to direct, many directors initiate their own projects and don't feel the need to pay 10% on work they feel they generate themselves. Broadway director, Jerry Zaks, brought up some good points for having an agent for other purposes:

As far as agents generating work, I don't think it works that way for directors. I appreciate the relationship I have with my agent. He's someone whose opinion I regard. He negotiates. I like to have people speak to him first. I have a terrible time saying 'no'. My agent screens the material and takes care of things I have no interest in doing.
Jerry Zaks/Director

On the other hand, Jim Cameron must have struck terror in the hearts of conglomerate agencies when he departed ICM:

Filmmaker James Cameron has given notice to ICM, his agency of 10 years, that from now on he will only

*work with the agency on a project-by-project basis. He will
now be represented by his attorneys.*

   *...Cameron said that he will not seek other
representation and his need for an agency had diminished.
"I'm in a different kind of situation, plus I'm wearing
dual hats because as a producer I need access to all the
major studios on an equal footing; I just thought, 'why pay
for a service that I'm not really using?' If it changes in the
future, I'll look again."*
   "Cameron Axes ICM"
   Anita M. Busch
   Daily Variety
   October 14, 1994

What Is an Agent Anyway?

The dictionary, which knows very little about show
business, has many definitions for the word *agent*.
By combining a couple, I've come up with: *A force
acting in place of another, effecting a certain result by
driving, inciting, or setting in motion; a go-between.*

   What does an agent do? Where do I find one?
Do I need an agent? How can I get an agent to talk to
me? What would I say to an agent? Are there rules of
behavior? How can I tell if an agent is a good agent?
When is the right time to look for an agent? What if
they all want to sign me, how can I choose the right
agent? What if no agent wants to sign me, do I have to
go back to Iowa? What will I tell my family?
   Tell your family that you are busy learning the
business. Tell them that when you get an agent you
will let them know, but that whether or not you have
an agent has nothing to do with the fact that you are
pursuing your dream. Being a director is about
directing, not about having an agent. Tell them that

---

you are happy and that making money will only be icing on the cake. Civilians (those who have never pursued a job in show business) and would be directors who have not "been on the street" yet, can't possibly empathize. They have no idea what any artist goes through in pursuit of employment and/or an agent. They're not going to understand anything except your name up on the screen or marquee in big letters where it says, "Directed by."

What Does An Agent Do?

In its simplest incarnation, the agent, acting on your behalf, sets in motion a series of events that result in your having a shot at a job. He gets you in the door for meetings, interviews and pitch sessions. He sends your reel around and gets people to view it. He searches for material you might be interested in. He makes sure buyers see your latest production, sends your reviews around and tells everyone that only you can make their next project a big success. Once you begin to be employed, he conceives a plan for your career. He adds to your credibility by his interest in you.

Many directors don't have agents, but most possess neither the contacts, information, nor the appetite for representing themselves over the long haul. In many instances, however, it is necessary to be your own first agent: finding your own first job(s), getting to know writers and producers, sending out mailings about your work, entering festivals, schmoozing and keeping up to date on what types of projects are being done.

Once you have a body of work, you'll have the option of concentrating on your directing and letting someone else shoulder the major portion of keeping your work visible. You will undoubtedly want an agent, manager or an industry lawyer's help with your career. But if you are smart, you will keep your hand in.

Besides getting the director's work seen, the agent must be prepared to negotiate a brilliant contract when the director is sold. That entails knowing all the contracts and all of the rules and regulations of DGA or the SSDC, as well as having an understanding of the marketplace and knowing what others at similar career levels are getting for similar jobs. He must then have the courage, style, and judgment to stand up to the buyers in asking for what is fair without giving in to the temptation to sell the director down the river financially in favor of his future relationship with the buyers or without becoming too grandiose and turning everyone off.

How Did He Get To Be An Agent?

Most of us have no idea how agents train for their jobs and, therefore, no basis on which to evaluate an agent intelligently. Do agents attend Agent University? The closest thing to AUs are the training programs/mail-rooms of the conglomerate initial agencies: CAA (Creative Artists Agency), ICM (International Creative Management), WMA (William Morris Agency) and UTA (United Talent Agency).

Whether or not he is involved in that process, the agent to covet has been getting to know the business, reading every screenplay, television script, play, novel; the written word in any form that might interest a buyer or teach an eager mind. He's watched the development of writers, actors, directors, and producers. He's apprenticed under some connected role model at another agency or at a studio. He's been meeting people on all levels of the business, networking, staying visible, and communicating. He's met producers, directors and vice presidents of development and he's cultivated relationships with them.

He, therefore, only represents those directors whose work he personally knows; so that when he tells a prospective buyer that he's found a brilliant new director who is perfect for an upcoming project because he is the next Andrew Davis or Jerry Zaks, the buyers will pay attention. Just like a director, an agent builds his credibility slowly, one step at a time.

■ *It's really very simple to describe what agents do— they work for their clients. They look for material, they read their clients' material and they set up deals for their clients. To do those tasks effectively, they also need to know everything that's going on around town.*
"Les Liaisons Dangereuses"
Charles B. Slocum
The Journal
June 1991

Time

The relationships agents build take time. To get people out and introduce them and get their name and work around takes a lot of time and effort. To follow up on it takes more time. It's a large investment. An agent who has done his homework is probably not going to be interested in you until you have done yours.

Make It Worth An Agent's While To Talk To You

Why would an agent talk to you? Have you spent years perfecting your work, directing, reading, writing, studying, observing directors you admire, watching film, television, reading classic screenplays, devouring television scripts, learning who you are, focusing your goals? Do you read the trades? Do you know who the buyers are who might be interested in what you specifically have to sell? Do you have your next project under your arm? Do you have the vocabulary with which to discuss the business with your prospective business partner? No? Well, get to it.

Franchised Agents

A director who is a member of The Directors Guild can represent himself anytime he wants. An agent conducting business for a director must have a license from the state and have signed an agreement with the DGA. That agreement is called a franchise. Just because an agent is franchised by the Guild is no guarantee that the agent is ethical, knowledgeable or effective. He probably is, but since this is an important decision, check him out.

So, Who's the Agent for You?

There are lots of agents around and making a choice can be confusing. Just because an agent has not yet established his credibility is no reason to turn up your nose, particularly if you are a little short in the credibility department yourself. Perhaps he's a star in process, just like you.

Any Agent?

As stated earlier, some famous directors have no agents listed in the DGA Directory, but list lawyers instead. Some list no one at all. When I asked agents if they felt no agent was better than a bad agent, I got a couple of interesting answers:

■ *If you have no one else wanting you to sign, carefully evaluate the situation. Does this person seem to be in a situation where he or she can help you? Look around the office. See who some of the clients are. Check them out a bit with other director friends. You can say to the agent, "Do I know any of your directors? This is exciting to me, who would I be with?" It's all in how you present yourself.*

Ken Sherman
Ken Sherman Agency
Los Angeles

■ *Directors can represent themselves or use an attorney or a manager. For an unknown director getting off the bus, I question the success rate of getting people to look at the reel without an agent. Generally the stock answer is, "We'll be happy to look at your reel if it comes from a franchised agent."*

Marty Shapiro
Shapiro-Lichtman
Los Angeles

■ *Is it better to have any agent rather than no agent? That's a hard question to answer. I'll confine* any agent *to a real person that the buying community recognizes as a valid agent, not someone who has an office on Moorpark and charges to read. Even if you are a beginner, you could call the Directors Guild and ask what they know about this agent. If you know anybody in the business that you can call and say, "Do you know anything about this person?" And if they say, "He's a nice person, but doesn't have much clout," then you have to decide. It all depends on how desperate you are. If it was me, personally, if I had faith in my own ability, I'd wait until there was somebody with more credibility—someone the community recognized as a valid agent who has been*

*able to sustain and earn a living for whatever—10-20
years. That should say something for them.*
Stu Robinson
paradigm
Los Angeles

■ *Well, 'hold out' for what? They could 'hold out'
indefinitely. What are they going to do while they are
holding out? The director's interest is in trying to direct so
that he can find someone who is willing to work with
him. He won't find entree in the marketplace because the
studios and the production companies won't talk to him
without an agent, so any agent is better than no agent.*
Marty Shapiro
Shapiro-Lichtman
Los Angeles

Wrap Up

Agent
a force acting in place of another, effecting a certain
result by driving, inciting, or setting in motion; a
go between.

Agent's Job
to become conduit to the buyers
to arrange meetings and interviews
to negotiate salary and billing
to have credibility, taste and courage

7   What Everybody Wants

Besides checking the marketplace for product, the smart businessperson takes the pulse of the buyer to determine how his offering will fare. If he is looking for an agent, it makes sense to find out what is on the agent's wish list. What is he looking for? Do you have to be a DGA member to arouse his interest? Is it enough to be industrious? Does your personality enter into the equation? Of course, the bottom line is, agents are looking for someone who will make them a lot of money. With that in mind, here are some of the things that agents say they are looking for.

We're more excited about a new theater director from New York than a director who has directed 20 episodes.
> Elliott Stahler
> *Kaplan Stahler*
> Los Angeles

Certainly an emotional reaction. But you have to be pretty steely-eyed about the direction. Are the characters directed well? Then, all the technical stuff, the lighting, the movement. I don't want to be conscious of the direction. I'm not interested in shots up people's nostrils. I want to concentrate on the movie, on the flow. If I have a happy experience, then to me, it is well directed.
> Stu Robinson
> *paradigm*
> Los Angeles

I look for someone who is talented, who works at their craft even when they are not employed, who is serious

*and will work at the career as well as the craft. He or she
can do that by going to parties, taking classes, having
lunches and generally trying to make themselves visible.
It's important to just get out there and meet people.*

Jonathan Westover
The Gage Group

*I have to look at their films and (even if it's
small) body of work and see that I think it's something
outstanding or different enough so that I can call my
producers and say, "You must look at this person. This
person is special!" Either it's someone who can do a lot on
a small budget and make it look expensive, or it's someone
who has a knack with actors and knows how to make that
little low-budget picture really shine.*

*Maybe it's someone who has a big background in
television, but wants to make the transition into features.
Maybe their old agent didn't want to make that effort and
maybe I will be the one to jump in there and say, "Okay, I
can move you into that area. I can give it my best shot."
Because I have been working so long, I have connections in
both film and television and with both low budget and the
bigger studio films.*

Michele Wallerstein
Wallerstein Kappleman
Los Angeles

*I look for originality, passion, an individual voice,
as well as someone who is a craftsman and is not afraid to
be different.*

Ken Sherman
Ken Sherman Agency
Los Angeles

*I only sign people whose talent, body of work and
general direction and taste coincide with mine. If the*

agent and client are really at odds with one another down that checklist, then you're not going to be productive in that relationship. You need to have a fundamental rapport just as you do in a relationship of any kind.

Michael Douroux
Douroux & Co.
Los Angeles

I want to know what kind of personal and professional maturity they demonstrate.

Elliot Stahler
Kaplan Stahler
Los Angeles

Money is not one of the top five considerations. More important is that they are realistic about where they are in the continuum of their career and they can't be insane. All anyone really wants is that they feel they are not going to be in the same place in their career in two years as they are now.

Bob Hohman
Richland/Wunsch/Hohman
Los Angeles

Most of us gravitate toward those clients who are easy to talk to because that communication helps to maintain our energy to fight the true battles.

"Les Liaisons Dangereuses"
The Journal
June 1991

An adult who is psychologically sound with whom you can spend 10 hours a day.

Bob Hohman
Richland/Wunsch/Hohman
Los Angeles

I look at their work. It's more a case of what you spark to, the choices the director is making every step of the way; the narrative skills, visual instincts, the ability to get a performance from their actors.

Michael Douroux
Douroux & Co.
Los Angeles

I want to know whether the director wants to do comedy, which is three-camera and tape or whether he/she wants to do film, which is completely different. That's one-camera film where it's mostly dramatic work. I think it's important to know who they know, what other directors they know, how focused they are, whether they have made a commitment to do either comedy or drama, whether they want to do features or movies of the week. These are all different careers although they do cross-over.

Each step is a different hurdle. If the ultimate goal is to do a feature, then the client may want to start out in drama, working in one-camera, as opposed to comedy. There's a certain perception about comedy directors that they haven't translated well to one-camera film careers.

Stephen Rose
Major Clients Agency
Los Angeles

I evaluate off the work, but I won't take someone who behaves antisocially. When a client goes in, he represents my agency. It's my name on that letterhead. He or she has to be someone I feel I can work with. I am not looking for the one shot, it has to be someone for the long haul.

Ken Sherman
Ken Sherman Agency
Los Angeles

I'm not in the business of breaking young movie directors and movie writers into the business. It's too labor intensive and the rewards both financially and emotionally are not there for me. That might change in a year, but I have too many clients in transition. Right now is about me reaping the rewards of "we did that together."

Bob Hohman
Richland/Wunsch/Hohman
Los Angeles

The Inexperienced Client

Recently, I had lunch with an agent who was discussing a new client who had just made a costly mistake. The client had written, directed and produced her own first effort with a partner and landed the agent. The agent sent it around and got the partners a meeting. When the development executive asked if there was material for the next venture, the director pitched her story. The exec offered two possibilities: she could give them $30,000 to go back and develop the project or the director and partner could go back and develop it on their own and then 'probably sell it to her for six figures.'

Instead of saying, "we'll think about it; our agent will talk to you," they opted for the 'six figures'. Now, neither the agent nor the director and partner can get the exec on the phone.

The agent is frustrated and the clients are disappointed. The agent might have been able to make a deal for the $30,000, plus some kind of 'back-end-deal' where the partners would get more money at each step of the process, thus keeping the project alive and giving them some money in the meantime.

This story exemplifies why agents are leery of first-timers. They can only 'start' so many new clients

---

and they don't want to use up their contacts on people who might stumble. Since it's difficult to plan for every eventuality, cover yourself and your agent by relying on their advice regarding any career decision. You don't have to follow the advice, but you should at least seek their informed viewpoint on how to conduct business. That expertise is one of the things you are paying for.

Things You Will Want to Consider

If you have your life in a fairly balanced state, an apartment, a reel, at least a nodding acquaintance with the economic perils of life as a director, some of the traits described by agents as being attractive, and are involved with other directors, it's time for you to begin serious research to determine the agent who is right for you.

Unfortunately, agents do not send out resumes in search of clients. Even if they are looking for clients (and they are all looking for the client who will make them wealthy and powerful beyond their dreams), agents don't send out a list of their training, accomplishments, and/or a personality profile. Beyond their list of clients (which is not, by the way, posted on their door), there is no obvious gauge of their worth; it is up to you to conduct an investigation of your future business partners.

You have already taken your first step; you bought this book giving you the benefit of my interviews with a cross-section of agents. I've asked about their background, looked at their client lists, queried clients, and in general conversed with anyone and everyone in the business who might have something informed to say about director's agents. I've also read everything I could get my hands on regarding agents and the way the business is conducted.

You should be having agent-related conversations with everyone you see. If you are just beginning and your contacts are limited to your peers, they will probably be just as uninformed as you, but trade information anyway. You never know where valuable information lurks.

Ask any other directors you can meet, any film school professors at universities, anyone you know. One of the jobs of professors is to refer their students to agents. Because the best agencies are constantly seeking to renew themselves by scouting new talent, they stay in touch with the universities. Agents attend screenings from time to time to see new writers and directors who come out of film school.

Jim Preminger
Jim Preminger Agency
Los Angeles

To help you make a more informed choice, I recommend a book called *Reel Power* written by Mark Litwak (William Morrow, New York). This book contains pragmatic information about how it really is to survive in the business and also has insightful material about what it takes to be an agent:

First, an agent must have the stamina to handle a heavy workload and be able to endure the frenetic pace in which business is conducted. "It's like working in the commodities pit," says William Morris agent Joan Hyler. "It's hectic," says agent Lisa Demberg, "because you can't do your job unless you're always on the phone, always talking to someone, or socializing with someone or trying to do business, or following up on the projects you've discussed."

"Great agents," says agent-turned-executive
Stephanie Brody, *"have enthusiasm and tireless energy.
And they must be efficient. The agent is juggling 30 phone
calls a day. He has to send out material, and follow up.
You have to be extremely well-organized."*

Second, agents must be able to cope with the
vicissitudes of the business. *"In a certain sense it's like
Dialing for Dollars,"* says William Morris agent Bobbi
Thompson. *"Each call may be the big money. You never
know. It's all a roulette wheel."* Third, an agent must be
an effective salesman. Fourth, agents must be able to
discern talent.

*"Many top agents are very aggressive in their
pursuit of deals; some would say ruthless."* Says a former
CAA agent, *"In order to be an extraordinarily successful
agent, you can't have any qualms about lying, cheating,
stealing and being totally into yourself."*

Mark Litwak
Reel Power
William Morrow, NY

Even though Bobbi Thompson said agenting is
sometimes like *Dialing for Dollars*, let's hedge our bets
with a little planning, intelligence and knowledge to
inform the luck by considering a few things that can
affect the hierarchy of representation.

The Numbers

The ratio of agents to clients is more crucial to
successful representation than the size of the office.
One person cannot effectively represent 100 people.
It's like going to the store and buying everything you
see. You can't possibly use everything, you're just
taking it out of circulation. Many agents believe a good
ratio is one agent to 20 to 25 clients. An agency with

four agents can do well by 100 or even 140 clients, but that really is the limit. Look closely at any lists that are extravagantly over this size; it's easy to get lost on a large list.

■ *Statistically, for every director that an agency would handle, there should be four or five writers. That's not even the ratio of development to production. Assuming that there are nine or ten projects developed for every movie, if you had ten directors who are film directors, you should probably be representing about 54 writers because the development production ratio is about that or more.*
Gary Salt
Paul Kohner, Inc.
Los Angeles

■ *We have managed to keep the size of the client list relatively small so that we can give a great deal of attention. I think for us, a ratio of 20 clients to one agent is actually a lot. Although I know that there are plenty of agents who represent 60-70 clients, I find for the kind of quality work that we do, that 20 each is a lot. We currently do have about 20 to 1, but we'd prefer less.*
Jim Preminger
Jim Preminger Agency
Los Angeles

Access

The dictionary defines access as "ability to approach" or "admittance." Because the conglomerate agencies have so many star directors on their lists, they have plenty of "ability to approach." If the studios, networks and producers do not return phone calls, they might find the agency retaliating by withholding the important actors that add credibility to the director's projects. CAA's real talent is not the deals the agency swings for Sydney Pollack, Harold Ramis and Oliver Stone. It's in attracting those successful directors.

Those agencies that get *A* for access—The William Morris Agency (WMA), International Creative Management (ICM), Creative Artists Agency (CAA) and United Talent Agency (UTA) do not usually offer career building services. These large corporations are there to cash in once credibility has already been established. Although it is true that star representation enhances some careers, it is not true in all cases.

Make sure you are seeking an agent you have the credits to attract. Rob Reiner's agent is probably not going to be interested. Make sure other clients on the agent's list are your peers. It's admirable to think big, but you must walk before you can run. Don't expect an agent who has spent years building his credibility to be interested in someone who just got off the bus. You must effectively agent yourself until you are at a point that a credible agent will give you a reading.

Stature

You don't have to be CAA to have stature. The dictionary defines stature as "level of achievement." So, Stu Robinson and Elliott Webb surely have more stature than some lowly agent at William Morris, but possibly not as much access—although once you have strong clients, the door opens pretty quickly.

■ *An agent is only as strong as the clients he or she represents.*
Elliot Webb
Broder.Kurland.Webb.Uffner
Los Angeles

Style

Stamina, the ability to discern talent, great selling ability, access, stature and a short list would seem to be all one might wish for in the ideal agent, but there is one more small item: personal style. Will you be able to stand talking to this person?

■ *There are some agents about whom you would say, this person is never going to be able to help me because I would never want this person going into a studio representing me. And there are some major agents in town you wouldn't want to have a cup of coffee with. Every agent works in his own way.*
Ken Sherman
Ken Sherman Agency
Los Angeles

A friend of mine left her agent because she felt he had not been doing a good job of negotiation. She switched agencies and got a hefty raise on her show. Unfortunately, she lost rapport and communication in the process and ended up leaving that agent as soon as her contract came up for renewal.

Some things are more important than others. Because directing is such a lonely occupation anyway (unless you are on staff), it's worthwhile to have someone you can bounce things off, so don't sell this attribute short.

Education

Just as some agents evaluate your unseen abilities by whether or not you have studied at UCLA, NYU or USC, finding out an agent's background and training can give you initial insights into who he is and what you might expect. Getting in on the ground floor with an agent ambitious enough to survive the grueling training at the large conglomerates may be an important way into the system for you.

Absorbing articles on this subject are: "The Players" by Lynn Hirshberg, *Vanity Fair*, January 1993; "Slaves of Wilshire Boulevard" by Andy Marx in the November/December 1991 issue of *Buzz* magazine; and "Is This the Next Mike Ovitz?" by Johanna Schneller, *GQ*, May 1992.

The articles are not only chilling reading, but they give a feeling for the vulnerability of beginning agents and insights into how to approach the power brokers of tomorrow.

I asked agents to switch places with the directors and tell me what directors should be looking for in an agent:

Evaluate the agent for rapport. Is the director comfortable talking to the agent? Be sure he is going with someone who has the time for him. Someone that doesn't have a lot of other new people at the same time. You can only walk in with a certain number of new people at a time. The director has to make a decision partly based on the accomplishments of the agency with other people in the past who have been in similar situations. If the agent has the kind of track record where he has taken other brand new people and been with them when their careers have been made, then that becomes a plus. What the director has to be terribly concerned with is that he doesn't get snowed and go with someone who is just giving him a line. Of course, he may never get to the point of having to do that because it is difficult, at best, for a new director to get in that door.

Marty Shapiro
Shapiro-Lichtman
Los Angeles

A good director's agent is out in the marketplace looking for good material that has the right elements attached for that director to step into.

Michael Douroux
Douroux & Co.
Los Angeles

The agent works for you. You don't want an agent who is conning you. You want someone who is honest. A lot of agents aren't. A lot of agents are. I don't want to ever get in a position where I have to figure out what I said yesterday. If you tell the truth, you don't have to do that.

Marty Shapiro
Shapiro-Lichtman
Los Angeles

I think that you want to feel that there is someone who is not just selling you on himself or herself to sign you and to keep you off the market, but that you have someone who is generally going to take an interest in you and your work for a long time. I would also pick someone I could stay with for a long time, not someone I can see going into the relationship, that I'm going to outgrow in two years time.

Jim Preminger
Jim Preminger Agency
Los Angeles

I think, first of all, you have to evaluate whether the agent understands the work. Is he simpatico in practical or abstract ways? You don't have to be crazy about your agent. After all, this is business; more important, does the agent understand you? Does he/she understand you as a person? Is this someone you can feel comfortable calling? Whom you will (hopefully) feel comfortable talking to on a regular basis?

Ken Sherman
Ken Sherman Agency
Los Angeles

My idea of success is sustenance. It's making it last and challenging yourself. You can have all the short term success in the world. You need a plan and you need a partner. My role is varied with each client. I'm not best friends with my clients. I'm very friendly with all of them, but we don't go on vacation. My relationship with some of them is quite formal and professional.

Bob Hohman
Richland/Wunsch/Hohman
Los Angeles

Choose the agent who has the highest enthusiasm for you. A company with five people is probably going to be stronger than a company with one person. But a company with 50 people is not necessarily stronger than a company with five people. The real question is, "Is your agent going to be saying your name every single day?" If the enthusiasm level is there, you are better off with the not-quite-so-important agent. If you are a brand new director, you are probably better off with The Gersh Agency than with Mike Ovitz.

Rima Greer
Above the Line Agency
Los Angeles

■ *If an agent turns you down, don't be depressed. It means that agent would not have been able to sell you anyway because you can't sell someone unless you have a passion. You should only want an agent who is passionate about your work. If you have passion, you can't stop.*
Raphael Berko
Media Artist Group
Los Angeles

Be Patient

Read the agent quotes and statistics carefully before you make judgments about which agent you might seek or even your readiness to attract an agent. Since the information is enhanced by an overview, make sure you have one. Then go back and read the agent listing section of the book again, taking notes. You'll learn their lineage, education, credits (clients), the size of their list and get some idea of their style.

If an agent interests you, check the index to see if the agent is quoted elsewhere in the book. Those quotes can give you a further clue as to how the agent conducts business, views the world and how compatible you might feel with him.

If all the names on the agent's list are stars and you are just beginning, that means this agent is too far along for you. If you read his dossier and don't recognize any of the clients' names, they may well be respected working directors whose names you don't happen to know. Ask questions. Perhaps it's an upcoming director whom you are unaware of. Maybe the agent is just starting and is building his list. If you are just beginning, perhaps you and the agent can build credibility together. It's worth a shot.

Copies of the Directors Guild Membership Directory are available by writing the DGA at 7920 Sunset Blvd., Los Angeles, CA 90046. It costs $25.00 plus $2.50 tax and postage. The Society of Stage Directors and Choreographers Directory of Members is available from the New York offices of SSDC for $7.00 at 1501 Broadway, 31st floor, New York, NY 10036. Members are listed with representation and key credits.

If you spend time leafing through the books, you will begin to get an overview of the agents and also become more knowledgeable about your fellow directors. Look for those agents you have noted. See who their clients are. You'll see famous directors with famous agents, but also some well-known clients represented by agents you might not have considered.

If you are a director of stature, you will be looking for an agent that lists some of your peers. Some fine agencies have opened in the last two or three years whose names may not be as well-known as older agencies, but who nonetheless are quite important. Usually, they are agencies started by agents who interned at larger offices, learned the business, groomed some clients, and left the agencies (frequently with some of the agency's choicest clients).

As you look at these lists, you are probably having fantasies about the large conglomerate agencies, but read Chapter 9 on Conglomerate/Star agencies before you form your final opinion. There are many pros and cons to star representation at various levels of one's career.

While you are salivating, remember that most stars come to star agencies after a struggling independent agent helped the director achieve enough stature and access of his own so that the conglomerate agent felt his interest was financially justified.

A friend of mine made her decision another way, passing an open door on the way to another agent's office, she overheard the agent at work on the telephone: *If my client's check is not on my desk by 5 p.m. this afternoon, I'm going to come over there and burn your office down.* She decided then and there that this was the agent she wanted.

If you are in the position of choosing, the question to answer is: who will provide the best opportunity for you to be gainfully employed in the business and beyond that, to build a real career?

When you have finished this book, you should have some idea of which agents appeal to you. Some names will keep coming up. Make a list. Even if you know you are only interested in Gary Salt or Marty Shapiro, target at least five names. You can't intelligently make a choice unless you do some research and meet your potential business partners face to face. Agent A may look great if you never have the chance to meet Agents B and C.

Ask advice from any show biz insiders (other directors, writers, producers, development executives) with whom you have formed relationships. Explain that you are agent shopping and that you would like advice about the names on your list and ask for any names they might like to add. Listen to their opinion but remember, producers and network honchos have a far different relationship with an agent than you will have. Make your own decision.

Wrap Up

The Ideal Client
has talent
displays a singular personality

---

exhibits professionalism
maintains mental health
is a DGA or SSD&C member
has a sense of style
is realistic about his career
can write

The Ideal Agent
is aggressive
has stature
has access
is enthusiastic about your work
shares your vision regarding your career
has an optimum ratio of directors to agents
has integrity
communicates with you
gives you guidance

Research
carefully read the information in this book
check The DGA Membership Directory
check SSD&C Directory of Members
consult your friends in show business
don't underestimate word of mouth

8   The Relationship

All your good work has paid off and you have now
been proposed to and you have accepted. You and
your agent are going to sign the piece of paper; you
now have representation.

As in all partnerships, each party assumes
certain responsibilities. And as in all relationships,
things go much smoother when both parties are
putting energy into the union. In the interest of
encouraging realistic expectations in director/agent
relationships, I asked several agents what they felt
was reasonable to expect in this alliance.

■   *You have a right to expect the best professional
judgement I can give you and the best professional
opinions I can give you with respect to your work, and
that within the limits of normal business practice and
normal working days, the agency is looking out for your
interests and promoting your work.*
Gary Salt
Paul Kohner, Inc.
Los Angeles

■   *Directors have a right to expect their agents to
return their phone calls, tell them the truth and work hard
on their behalf.*
Maggie Field
The Maggie Field Agency
Los Angeles

■   *Right or wrong, when represented by an agent, you
are banking on their experience and their opinion. It
doesn't mean that it's gospel. It just means it's the best they
can give you at this time. They can be wrong and*

sometimes they are wrong. But more often than not, they ought to be right and so, long term, you want to feel that the agent is a sounding board for you and a better professional sounding board than your relatives or your friends or your wife or your kids or your next door neighbor.

Gary Salt
Paul Kohner, Inc.
Los Angeles

Communication is very important. You call or I'll call.

Stu Robinson
paradigm
Los Angeles

What we try to do is to successfully maximize a client's career over a long period of time which will help him or her become both financially and creatively secure. Being financially secure provides a certain power, the power to say "no" to a project or having a range of work options to choose from. An agent's power is in his ability to say "no" or "yes" on behalf of his client.

Elliot Webb
Broder.Kurland.Webb.Uffner
Los Angeles

It's most important that you'll be told the truth about what's going on. People should remember that unlike lawyers who get their $300 per hour whether their advice is right or stinks, the agent doesn't get anything unless he's successful. People should bear that in mind. That doesn't mean that you can't ever say anything because the guy hasn't made any money off you. I think if I were a client, I would say, "Look, I'm entitled to honest direct communication, I'm entitled to having my phone *call returned. And I'm entitled to occasional evaluation periods as to 'Are we doing the right thing? What can we do to change it?' Stuff to me that is common sense.*

Stu Robinson
paradigm
Los Angeles

To accurately assess where the client is in the continuum of their career. To honestly tell the person where they are. To evaluate whether the person heard you. To figure out how to get from where you are to where you want to go. To keep the client growing. If you don't do 1-2-3, it won't work. You need a plan.

Bob Hohman
Richland/Wunsch/Hohman
Los Angeles

The power in Hollywood is money. It's true. Every powerful person in Hollywood is wealthy. There is a certain power in the ability not to be needy.

Elliot Webb
Broder.Kurland.Webb.Uffner
Los Angeles

I also asked what was too much to expect:

Too much is calling three times a week to ask the same question. I'd call the agent every two to two and a half weeks just to say "Hello, here I am. What? Tell me something, anything?"

Stu Robinson
paradigm
Los Angeles

Of course, it goes both ways. Agents have expectations, too:

■ *Communication is very important. We don't want clients not communicating – sitting and brooding. I don't mind if a client calls once every two weeks and says, "Hey, what can I do?"*
Stu Robinson
paradigm
Los Angeles

■ *His honest opinion. Genuine excitement and enthusiasm from that client in a piece of material. That's what's going to fuel them through what is always a difficult process under the best of circumstances. Film-making is difficult. The thing that keeps the director in the game throughout is the passion for the material. When times are tough and days are dark and everything is going wrong, it's that mind's eye that brought him into the process to begin with that keeps him going.*
Michael Douroux
Douroux & Co.
Los Angeles

■ *I expect the client to continue to toot horns any which way they can. And I'm talking about people who have been working in the business for a long time. The more successful you get as a writer or director, the more contacts you have, the more people who appreciate you. So theoretically, the job gets easier for the agent as the career develops. Certainly at the beginning stages, you have to do everything you can. I don't mean in conflict with what your agent is doing, but in concert.*
Stu Robinson
paradigm
Los Angeles

A Synergistic Relationship

Synergy is one of my favorite words. The thought that
in some instances two plus two can equal five because
two components complement each other elegantly,
appeals to my feelings that anything is possible. The
possibilities that exist when an agent and client are
both motivated above and beyond the call of duty is
actually a necessity if you want to be one of the 5% to
10% of the DGA that works regularly.

*A lot of talent doesn't understand their relative
importance to the business. We believe that this is a
business like any other business and that our job is to focus
and manage the career, to explain the business to the
talent. Yes, we recognize you have talent. Now, what do
you want to do with that?*
Elliot Stahler
Kaplan Stahler Agency
Los Angeles

90%-10%

The whole concept of 90%-10% bears looking into.
How many of us have resented our agents when we
have been requested for a job and all the agent had to
do was negotiate? In fact, if all our jobs were requests,
would we just have a lawyer negotiate and do away
with the agent altogether? Or is the support and
feedback worth something? What about all the times
he may send a reel and/or talk about us and *not* get an
appointment so we never knew about it? And all the
appointments we went on and didn't get the job? That
costs him money that we frequently don't consider
when we're whining about his shortcomings.
Maybe the whole thought process about agents

is incorrect. Agents really don't get you work. Your work gets you work. Not just your ability to function well as a director, but the ability to function well as a human being—because in the end, that is what influences your work more than anything else. John Frankenheimer said it: *He* was the one stopping himself because of his own personal problems. You can change agents or mates or clothes sizes to try to make yourself feel better, but the fact is that we all have to experience our lives in order to move to the next place.

Life changes are reflected in our work and ability to deal with other people. If one commits to experiencing the evolutionary process instead of fighting it, the transition occurs more quickly.

Paul Schrader made an interesting comment about how the changes in his life have influenced his work:

Well, I'm a middle-aged man with a family. I think the existential hero has pretty well run his course for the moment. He's been around for 100 years and, I don't know, maybe I'll go back to him one day. But after Light Sleeper, *I started to feel that maybe, you know, it's time to hang him up for a while — the lonely man in his room. I'm just moving on. It comes with living with children in the suburbs, and being a different age, and having a different sense of morality.*
"Exorcising His Dark Side"
Daniel Cerone
The New York Times
August 13, 1994

So, although you can hope that agents are going to use their contacts, creativity, status and energy to move you toward your goals, they do get only 10% of the money. You will have to do more for your 90%

than show up on the set. In every area of the business, acquiring the chance to use your talent is frequently as consuming as the job itself. If you can remember that, not only will you accomplish more, you'll be a lot less cranky.

Jonathan Westover at The Gage Group quoted his mentor, Dan Richland: "Why would you leave 100% of your career to someone who only gets 10% of your money?"

Ways You Can Help

Reinvent yourself. The easiest way to reinvent yourself is to have a script of your own that you control and you can decide what happens with it. I think it's important for artists to reinvent themselves every 3 to 5 years anyway.

Dean Pitchford is someone who has reinvented himself. Dean was an Academy Award-winning lyricist for Fame. *In 1984 he wrote a hugely successful screenplay,* Footloose, *followed by other successful screenplays. And in 1990, he decided that he was going to become a director. He entered the Discovery Program, and out of 600 people, he was one of five who were picked. He did a movie that turned out terrifically. Then he got another film at HBO called* Blood Brothers.

Bob Hohman
Richland/Wunsch/Hohman
Los Angeles

A director can't go home and write a script. Directors need to flex their muscles all the time, so I really encourage my movie directors to be open-minded about the episodic television business, about the cable and network two-hour movie business, because I really see the television business expanding. The sci-fi channel just came on. Lifetime and TNT and Showtime are all doing their own films now. I'm all about keeping people working.

Bob Hohman
Richland/Wunsch/Hohman
Los Angeles

Divorce?

Unfortunately, not all relationships work out. If your agent won't return your calls, if he's been dishonest or is not getting your name around, you may want to leave him.

In the rules of The Directors Guild, if a director has had no work in 90 days, he can void his contract with an agent by sending a letter to the agent plus copies to the Guild, advising them of Rider D, Paragraph 3. This is also called *The 90-Day Clause*. (See Glossary).

Maybe you and your agent have different ideas regarding your potential. This is something that should have been ironed out before the contract was signed, but sometimes that conversation comes later in the relationship.

Many directors leave their agents because their careers have changed and they feel they can be better serviced by agents with different sets of contacts. Perhaps your level of achievement in the business has risen. You have now, through brilliance or possibly a lucky break, become a director with more stature than your agent. This is very possible if fortune has just smiled on you.

It can happen the other way, too, of course. One minute you're hot and the next moment you're not. You didn't necessarily do anything so differently to get un-hot. Frequently getting hot works the same way.

There are different points of view, but the bottom line is that the director/agent relationship is just like any other relationship: as long as it's mutually rewarding, everyone is happy. When it's not, things must change.

Directors and agents seek each other because they see money making potential. Thirty five perfectly credible agents may pass on you and then agent number thirty six may fall in love, send your reel to the right place where the right script is waiting and you are suddenly a star.

At a smaller agency, being warm or even cold won't necessarily make you persona non grata, but at the big agencies, it might be difficult for you to get your agent on the phone.

■ *The business is high stakes. It's easy for another agent to whisper in a client's ear. It was done as far back as the apocryphal story about agent Swifty Lazar telling Humphrey Bogart, "I could get you four deals in a day" and he did and he got Bogart as a client. Even then, there was a tremendous amount of competition to represent talented people because that's where the strength is.*
Elliot Webb
Broder.Kurland.Webb.Uffner
Los Angeles

The larger agencies are not in the business to handle less profitable jobs, so they either drop you or their lack of interest finally tells you that you're no longer on their level. This is the moment when you might be sorry you left that small agent who worked so hard to get you started and engineered the big break for you. Will he want to see you now? He might. He might not. It depends on how you handled it when you left.

I asked agents if they ever dumped clients and if so, why?

▪ *Drop clients? When it's a mutual thing. We have a responsibility to the director, so we try for a period of time and if we haven't been able to help them, we tell them if they feel that they would like to get someone else, we'd certainly understand. We wouldn't throw somebody out. We have dropped people when they have been abusive. We are in a highly charged business and we really don't have to tolerate that.*
    Marty Shapiro
    Shapiro-Lichtman
    Los Angeles

Maybe you want to leave your agent because the magic has gone out of your marriage, just as the magic can go out of a traditional marriage if both partners don't put energy into it. And just as in marriage, it's always a better deal to try to rekindle the relationship, if possible. You were in love once, what went wrong?

▪ *It's a harder job with someone at an earlier stage of his career because he is sort of an unknown property, but it can also be the most rewarding. They forget quickly and leave you. It's hard. A lot of people don't know how bad an agent feels when he loses a client.*
    Stephen Rose
    Major Clients Agency
    Los Angeles

If you are both willing to save the relationship, that process will take a lot less energy than the "just learning to get to know each other" period involved in a new relationship.

Don't Wait Until It's Too Late

If something is bothering you, speak up. Confrontation comes easily to very few people. We all want to be liked and it's hard to challenge the situation. If you are unhappy and feel you will never work again, call your agent and tell him you are concerned. He knows as well as you that you are not working. Ask him if there is anything you can do. Ask if he has heard any negative feedback.

Whatever you do, don't just start interviewing other agents. You owe it to yourself and to your agent to talk before you get so angry that it is impossible for you to continue the relationship. If you have a conversation early on, perhaps both of you can find some way to remedy the situation. If you can't, at least he will have some idea of where you are coming from later when you are ready to leave.

Telling/Shopping

Before you start looking for a new agent, you must make a decision about telling your current agent you are going to leave. Most directors are hesitant not only because they are embarrassed and guilty, but also because they feel the agent might stop submitting them and they would be left unrepresented while shopping.

First of all, I doubt the agent would want to forego the commissions due on any new jobs.

Second, if he wants to keep you, this is his chance to demonstrate you are making a mistake and he really *is* the best agent in the world, after all.

Every agent I questioned said they would never leave a client without representation while he was shopping.

Another plus for telling your agent is that by

being forthright, you demonstrate to prospective partners that you conduct business in a truthful manner. Believe me, people notice. I took my own advice and was not only invited to return if things didn't work out, but the agent told me how much he appreciated my candor. It was a difficult subject to bring up, but the experience left me and the agent both feeling good about each other.

Leavetaking

If it is too late for a talk or you talked and it didn't help, at least leave with a little class. Even though it might be uncomfortable, get on with it. There is no need for long recriminations. No excuses. Not "My wife thinks..." or "My manager thinks..." No, it's "I've decided that I am going to make a change. I appreciate all the work you have done for me. I will miss seeing you, but it just seems like the time to make a change. For whatever reason, it's just not working. I hope we'll see each other again."

Whatever. You don't need to be phony. If you don't appreciate what the agent has done and don't think he's done any work, just skip it. Talk about the fact that you think the relationship is not, or is no longer, mutually rewarding. Be honest and leave both of you with some dignity. You may see this person again. With some distance between you, you might even remember why you signed with him in the first place. Don't close doors.

If you are leaving because your fortunes have risen, it is even harder. The agent will *really* be upset to see you and your money leave. Also, your new found success has probably come from his efforts as well as yours. But if you are really hot and feel only CAA or ICM can handle you, leave you must. Tell your agent you wish it were another way, but the vicissitudes of the business indicate that at a certain career level, CAA and their peers have more information, clout, and other stars to bargain with and you want to go for it.

If you handle it well and if your agent is smart, he will leave the door open. This has happened to him before and it will happen to him again. That doesn't make it hurt less, but this is business. He will probably just shake his head and tell his friends you have gone crazy: "This isn't the same MaryI always knew. It's gone to her head."

The agent has to find some way to handle it just as you would if he were firing you. It will not be easy to begin a new business relationship, but you are hot right now and the world is rosy.

Wrap Up

Director Expects
communication
honesty
market overview
feedback
taste/judgement
career guidance
synergistic relationship
contract negotiation skills

Agent Expects
that you won't embarrass him at meetings
professional behavior
synergistic relationship
the client to continually reinvent himself

Mutual Grounds for Divorce
dishonesty
abuse of any kind by anybody

sudden career change
lack of communication
differing goals
personality differences

Generally
speak to agent before shopping
don't burn bridges

9   Star/Conglomerate Agencies

If you are really *hot* and Mike Ovitz is buying your dinner, could you resist? Should you? After all, Creative Artists is the most powerful agency in the world. Wouldn't *everybody* rather have CAA?

There are agencies in town who have great strength in representing directors. Now, that strength can also be a liability. A lot of directors who are young and are coming up feel that they don't want to be the fifth name or the eighteenth name on a list that is headed by Barry Levinson. On the other hand, that's a bit of a mistake too because that means that they are presuming that they and Barry Levinson are competing for the same shots. I'm not sure that's true. The mere fact that an agency is representing twelve top directors doesn't necessarily mean that they're not going to represent a young guy well and competently.

The question is, in the long term, is there long-term benefit from these associations? Or, if he has to go head to head with other top directors, should he be at the same place? It's a very hard question to answer. I can't answer it. I've never been a client, so I don't know. I know what people tell me, but that may be sour grapes or disgruntlement because sooner or later everyone thinks their agent is not doing enough for them; they could be doing more, they could be doing better. Is anybody ever working enough? Or making enough?
Gary Salt
Paul Kohner, Inc.
Los Angeles

A lot of the people that I am representing were at bigger places (CAA, William Morris, etc.). Let's say that your agent left the business and you have been at a nice small place for a long time where you have had lots of attention. All of a sudden, you are faced with a decision: "Gee, I wasn't unhappy with my representation, but this person no longer exists." The dog and pony show that these big places do (and I was at a big agency and I used to do it) is, "Here we are, we are all powerful and all connected and look at all the information we have (and they pull out reams of paper) and we represent all these movie stars and we'll package you with our people and we'll use our clout to get you this and that."

For 75% of the list, that's heinous bullshit, because it's impossible to spread that wealth around. It's clout because it's only used on a few people. That's why they call it clout. It's impossible to service 150 directors well. CAA has a gigantic directors list and I would say they do an incredible job for about 25% of that list. For the rest of them, I hope it works out.

The point is, that with some people, they wake up one day and say, "Gee, I'm here at this big agency and I keep getting shuffled from one agent to another. How do I access that clout?" And they decide they need a little more personal representation. Large agencies give very personal representation to about 25% of their clients. The rest of them are dangling.

A lot of the people that I've gotten into business with aren't seduced by the clout thing. I've been here at the party long enough that I can get anybody on the phone and, frankly, if a client of mine is a long shot on a project, he has a much better chance with me because I'm only calling about him. I'm not calling about 10 people with bigger names, or whatever, or 10 equally long shot names.

Most people in the business are not operating at the highest levels. They're having good careers and making a good living off it. What you need to make sure is that you are maintaining that level and that you have someone who is keeping you fresh and keeping you out there. It *takes very personal focused representation.*

I don't represent Bernardo Bertolucci and I don't represent Sydney Pollack. While I would love to represent both of them, I probably never will. I'm very realistic about who I am as an agent. I represent a very nice high end writer and director base, but they are all people that I feel some sort of parity with as people. I'm very proud of and very comfortable with the people I represent and I think we deal with each other as equals. I always approach it that I'm able to give them the time that they deserve or I wouldn't have taken them on.

Bob Hohman
Richland/Wunsch/Hohman
Los Angeles

A lot of people go to big agencies out of fear. They *stay there out of fear. They feel if they are not in that arena, they're not in the game. Then, once they get there, they become very disenchanted and very disillusioned pretty quickly. Yet they don't leave for fear that some sort of pox will be put upon them and then they will never work again or it will be some sort of admission of failure to leave such a big agency. The big agencies are geared to service certain situations and, obviously, very well. You can't take anything away from them in that respect, but they are not right for all situations and all situations are not right for them.*

Michael Douroux
Douroux & Co.
Los Angeles

I'm real opinionated about the agency business. I *know a lot about it. It's the only thing I've ever done... I'm very happy being in a small agency environment. The primary difference between a big agency and a small agency is that it's impossible for a big agency not to have its own agenda. Some portion of the clients end up serving that agenda, whether that is in their best interests or not. Small agencies are generally about the clients interests and desires. It's far more client driven. The big agency has a big overhead, whereas we have a very contained, intelligently drawn overhead, which is fairly easy to meet. We are recession proof, whereas a big agency isn't. My partners and I feel that we have enough successful clients, and that there is always enough prosperity that if you say, "You know, I want to take off a year and write a book," we're able to say "good for you," assuming that you have the financial wherewithal to do that. It really is a marriage relationship where it is, hopefully, two adults trying to behave like adults with each other. If you want to do something that isn't financially remunerative, then that's your decision. It's far more about your desire than it's about us needing to use your talents.*

Bob Hohman
Richland/Wunsch/Hohman
Los Angeles

Obviously, I've chosen to spend my life in a small setting. Part of that is based on the fact that I'm most comfortable in a smaller setting. So if a writer or director chooses to go with us, they probably choose us because they think they won't get lost here. It's a matter of individual choice. Some clients like the razzle dazzle of the larger agency with just the sheer amount of activity and the access to whatever those resources are.

Jim Preminger
Jim Preminger Agency
Los Angeles

There are certain kinds of clients who want to be with us. The thing that separates the wheat from the chaff is that I think we are virtually with a very realistic group of people. We have very few virgins. We've all been around for a while. We are in the business with a lot of adults who know what representation is all about. We have a relatively small practice. We are not in the volume business. We don't take people on just for money. It wouldn't be worth it. We have to have a real affinity for the person's work.

Bob Hohman
Richland/Wunsch/Hohman
Los Angeles

What's the Best Decision?

I guess we've all heard the joke about the director who killed four people, ran over a baby, bombed a building, then ran across the street into The William Morris Agency, and was never seen again. It's pretty much the quintessential story about the wisdom of being signed by a big conglomerate agency.

The whole question of whether the large, star-level, conglomerate agency is the best place to be is pretty heady. As you progress, you'll find that heady is the perfect word for the dilemma. Both sides of this issue have validity.

Buyer friends of mine at the highest level tell me that large agencies who package, routinely sell out clients who command less $$$ even if that client would be better for the project. High rent, you know.

Fresh off the most commercially successful foreign film ever in the United States, Like Water for Chocolate, *director Alphonso Arau probably figured his agency, CAA, would use its clout to make it easier for him to snag a hot star for his new English language movie,* A Walk in the Clouds. *Since Keanu Reeves has ended up with the lead...Arau doesn't exactly appear to have been mistreated.*

But, filmmakers around town who are wary of CAA's machinations have been buzzing with the rumor that the monster agency "helped" their director client out by earlier convincing their client Brad Pitt that he "shouldn't" do the part. Then, they promoted Schindler*-hot client Ralph Fiennes for the role while insisting he be paid the $1,000,000 they said he's been offered to appear with Denzel Washington in* Devil in a Blue Dress—*all of which was supposedly just a ploy to get Fiennes that fee for the film they actually wanted him to do. It was at this point that CAA brought in client Reeves.*

"Casting About"
Yvette Mason
Movieline
July 1994

I hate to say it, but research leads to the conclusion that the star agencies (CAA, ICM, WMA, UTA) have the most power, the most information, and the best likelihood of getting you in for meetings and ultimately jobs, if someone there who is powerful and/or hungry believes in you.

I spoke with WMA agents, Jeff Hunter and Gene Parseghian. Once merely distinguished, tasteful, successful, mid-level agents, they created their own conglomerate, Triad before they merged with WMA. Since they had experienced the pain of helping build clients' careers and watching them move on to a conglomerate, I asked if from their new vantage point, they felt the actor had made a better career decision.

Yes, I resented it, but I knew it then.
Jeff Hunter
William Morris Agency
New York

■ *Yes, I understand why they would leave another agent. I can't understand why they would leave me.*
    Gene Parseghian
    William Morris Agency
    Los Angeles

Conglomerates do have more power and information. The questions are: What will they do with it? And, do power and information compensate for lack of personal attention?

The power of the large agencies comes from the star actors, writers and directors. When you have Andrew Davis, Penny Marshall, Hal Prince, Robert Zemeckis and Sydney Pollack on your list (plus hundreds of other big names) you have the attention of the buyers. The Catch-22 is, if you are Davis or Zemickis, you really don't need those agencies (because you are the power) and, if you're not one of those folk, you are mainly filler.

APA, though a definite conglomerate is not really even one of the 'big four,' but my experience touring their library was more than a little intimidating. More scripts than I have read in my lifetime stand cover sheet to cover sheet begging for attention. All are scripts somewhere on the development path. APA agents have access to that information and they have access before the package is even completed. They can tell you today to stop developing that project about O. J. Simpson because that script is already in pre-production.

■ *When I was in a one-room office on 57th Street in New York, I was as powerful as anyone, if I believed in someone. I could get them in anyplace, because I wouldn't take 'no' for an answer. I believe if someone works out of a phone booth on Hollywood and Vine, if they believe in*

---

you, they can get you in as quickly as the strongest agent in town.

    John Kimble
    William Morris Agency
    Los Angeles

Gene Parseghian (WMA) even confessed to me that there are days he wishes he still had a small office with three or four people and 20 clients, tops.

As I mentioned elsewhere in the book, conglomerates are not equipped to handle clients who are not making a lot of money. They have a big overhead. They are not interested in building careers.

And since so much money is involved, the media is ever vigilant in reporting the adventures of ICM, WMA and CAA. It's not difficult to chart their progress in the popular press and in show biz books. Tracking the machinations of the power struggles among the conglomerates is not only entertaining, it's instructive. The following is quoted from a chapter devoted to CAA (*The Rise of CAA*) in the excellent book by Mark Litwak called *Reel Power.*

More powerful than Sylvester Stallone, Steven Spielberg or Barry Diller, the most influential person in Hollywood is not a star, a director or a studio head. While his name is rarely in the news media and he never gets a screen credit, everyone who matters in the industry knows who he is. He is assiduously courted by producers and studio heads alike, because they need his cooperation in order to gain the services of the best writers, stars and directors in the industry. He is Mike Ovitz, the president of Creative Artists Agency.

CAA does not have the bureaucracy of William Morris or the bickering of ICM. It has restrained its growth and carefully chosen its agents with an eye toward their ability to work well together. CAA partner Martin Baum says his agency is successful because its agents put the welfare of the agency ahead of their own interests. "The policy of this company from its inception has been that we all profit if one succeeds." It has been the first time that there has been a total sublimation of the individual ego for the betterment of the group.

The rise of CAA is a particular sore point with William Morris, where the original CAA partners learned the business. The partners were considered the best and brightest and when they left Morris, it was a traumatic experience for the proud agency. "It was like their sons left." said WMA agent Debra Greenfield. There had never been a mass defection before.

Mark Litwak
Reel Power
William Morrow & Co
New York

In 1991 and 1992, there was an enormous shifting of power among the star agencies. CAA became even more powerful when Mike Ovitz, besides representing seemingly all the big players in the business acted as the power broker in the buyout of Universal Films by the Japanese company, Matsushita. The other pivotal event was detailed in the August 1991 issue of *Premiere* magazine.

It didn't sound like big news at first— just a terse announcement in the trades that senior William Morris agent Toni Howard had ankled her post for International Creative Management, taking with her such star clients as Anjelica Huston, James Spader, and Jason Robards. But a week later, when Elaine Goldsmith and Risa Shapiro joined her, taking Julia Roberts, Tim Robbins, and Andie MacDowell, it began to look serious.

"The Case of the Ankling Agents"
Premiere Magazine
August 1991

ICM now has a much more even standing with CAA in the quantity and quality of their stars. Granted the stars we are talking about here are actors, but we all know that star actors are only the first line of ammunition for an agency. If you've got the star actors, you make it a point to have the star writers and directors.

In the Fall of 1992, seeking to recover from previous losses, The William Morris Agency managed to come to a long rumored acquisition of Triad, in order to recoup some star power. At the same time, boutique powerhouse InterTalent threw in the towel when its president, Bill Block, returned to the fold at ICM. Other principals from InterTalent fanned out to various other agencies, most notably United Talent.

■   *Capping a historic week for Hollywood's agencies and ending four months of secretive negotiations, the 95-year old William Morris Agency has acquired Triad Artists in an aggressive move to help resuscitate its motion picture business and reinstate its image as an entertainment powerhouse.*
"William Morris Bulks Up on Triad"
Claudia Eller
Daily Variety
October 10, 1992

■   *After protracted negotiations, International Creative Management officials confirmed yesterday that InterTalent Agency topper Bill Block and 12 of his associates have joined ICM as expected.*
The 38-year-old Block—who is returning to ICM

after four years of running his own shop—has been installed as head of the agency's West Coast office, with day to day responsibilities for the motion picture and television areas.

After heading the agency's literary department for four years, Block ankled ICM in February 1988 to launch ITA (InterTalent) with Creative Artists Agency counterparts David Greenblatt and Judy Hofflund.

Just over a week ago, in order to bolster its agent and talent ranks, mid-size United Talent Agency signed deals with former ITA partners Hofflund, J.J. Harris and David Schiff.

"Block, 12 Others Join ICM"
Claudia Eller
Daily Variety
October 23, 1992

The pecking order: CAA, ICM, WMA and UTA. You'd probably be thrilled to be in the company of the names on any of their lists. There are, of course, stars at many other agencies in town, other than the conglomerates. Check The DGA and SSD&C directories to see who's where.

If one of the star/conglomerate agencies beckons, you can be sure they will do it with great style: limos, fancy restaurants and other appealing lures.

As I spoke to agents, I kept hearing them say over and over: "I got this person started. Just when it was all paying off, CAA or ICM came with the limos, the flowers. The client left. Why?"

I'm reminded of something Elliot Stahler said when I asked about clients changing agents: "Some clients demonstrate a certain amount of immaturity through their susceptibility to other agents telling them what they will do for them, etc."

It may be immature and it may be a mistake,

but many actors, writers and directors dream of growing up to be represented by CAA or ICM and consider it the mark of success. Even if they don't stay, they can say they've been there.

As in other important decisions like whom to marry, which doctor or lawyer to hire and whether or not to have elective surgery, you can only collect data, use your research and instincts and make a decision based on what is important to you. When all is said and done, limos not withstanding, do you want a family member or do you want a corporation?

So there you are. My final vote is for a prestigious, successful, tasteful mid-size agency. Of course, no one has plied me with limos and flowers, either.

Wrap Up

Conglomerates
have more information
command more power
have access to more perks
can package effectively
give less personal attention to many clients
provide less support in times of duress
their advice is corporate, less personal
have a big overhead
lose interest when you are not in demand
unless you are on the A list, you are probably filler

Independent Agencies
will probably be more impressed with you
may work harder for you
will probably be more accessible
will probably give more personal attention
more likely to be there through thick or thin

10   First Aid

Life in the business is a constant challenge. Directors are rejected and think they will either never work or never work *again*. Everyone in a free lance business experiences this at one time or another. This last chapter is filled with ideas, words of wisdom, institutions and information that seem to offer help and inspiration. Roger Corman's method of product scrutiny struck me as a particularly good idea.

■   *The crew and staff went to a sneak preview in Glendale and the whole theater saw what we were up to. Then, as Roger often asked us to do, we all went back to the office and everybody had to write a review as if we were working for* The Saturday Review *or* The New York Times. *And these were hard reviews, man. Nothing was held back. You could take shots at the art direction, sound, acting, story—whatever. There were no excuses like, "Sure, but they only had two days." Uh-uh. We spent an hour writing them up and if you weren't finished, you talked it through. Roger, I must say, had a thick skin for this, but he used the notes both to make changes in the current picture and to learn for the next. He could take it all, any of it. The notices we wrote on* The Little Shop of Horrors *were great ones, better than anything* The Saturday Review *could come up with.*
>   *How I Made a Hundred Movies*
>   *in Hollywood and Never Lost a Dime*
>   Roger Corman/Jim Jerome
>   Dell Publishing, 1990

■   *I think the people who sustain success are good listeners who really know what they want. They are people who let me know what they want and I*

help them do it. X% is genes.
>   Bob Hohman
>   *Richland/Wunsch/Hohman*
>   Los Angeles

"If you're a person who likes to define why you can't do something and looks for blame and feels victimized, you will be. If you're the kind of person who sees no obstacles, who wants to have a good time, that's better," says Caryn Mandabach, President of Carsey-Werner.
>   "Breaking Barriers"
>   Roberta G. Wax
>   *EMMY*/October 1994

Art comes from art. Art is a reaction to art. Rembrandt didn't start in a vacuum. He just was better than everybody else. A novelist reads novels. You have to drown yourself in this information, reading screenplays— why a scene worked, how these people are interesting, how the writer chose to describe the scene. Watch movies.
>   Lynn Pleshette
>   *Pleshette & Green*
>   Los Angeles

Agents don't bill by the hour. They only get commissions when people work and earn money. Therefore the fundamental relationship is economic. It's so clear cut and it's so pure and uncontaminated by distractions like "Do I like him?" Who cares? It's irrelevant. Who cares if I get Christmas cards or not? The only thing the agent is entitled to is his 10%. The uncontaminated relationship is economic and, therefore, it is about as honest a relationship as you're ever going to get, because nothing is served by the agent prevaricating to his client. If I was looking at a really good piece of film, why would I

pretend it is not?
Gary Salt
Paul Kohner, Inc.
Los Angeles

■ *I've had the good fortune to work with some very talented people and I've also had the good fortune to work with some real hacks. There's something to be learned from both. From the hacks, you learn how to do things quickly; if you're in a bind, there's a basic thing you can do to get out of it. From the talented people, you learn inspiration. You learn what to do and what not to do. I've had 15-18 years observing people doing what I wanted to do.*
John Kretchmer/*Director*

■ *A director needs patience because 50% of the job is how the director works with actors and 50% of the job is technical ability. I think that directors sometimes lose sight of the fact that they need to make their cast and their crew comfortable and make it as enjoyable and pleasant an experience as possible.*
Rima Greer
Above the Line Agency
Los Angeles

■ *Theater managers are very eager to find those people that they think can direct, because obviously it's an enormous responsibility. Doing it once gets people's attention, doing it twice gets them to perk their ears up and doing it again encourages people to send scripts and makes for being able to plan your life in a way that I certainly could never do as an actor.*
Jerry Zaks/*Director*

■ *Make sure you are the dumbest person on the set.*
Surround yourself with brilliant people who really know
what they are doing—who make you look great.
Bob Hohman
Richland/Wunsch/Hohman
Los Angeles

Director Chris Columbus puts director career
opportunity in perspective:

■ *I take a very long view. I look at the works of*
early directors I admire, like John Ford and Howard
Hawks and Capra—these guys had a chance to learn their
craft, they were directing three pictures a year. Us new
guys, we start and we're doing maybe one picture every
two years, and suddenly that first picture, that second
picture—everybody's looking at it as if: "Is this going to be
the next Citizen Kane?" *You can't put a disclaimer at the*
beginning of the film that says, "I'm not declaring that
this is the best film ever made. I'm declaring that I've
finally gotten a chance to direct."
"The New World of Chris Columbus"
F. X. Feeney
Movieline
November 1992

■ *People who make it are people who don't give up.*
John Kretchmer/*Director*

■ *There are an awful lot of creative and talented*
people out there. Unfortunately, it's not just talent that
brings success. There's luck, timing, persistence, and a
whole variety of things that enter into it. You can't get
discouraged. You have to have patience and you can't
expect it to happen overnight. If one, ten, or even twenty
agents don't respond to your work, keep trying. Somebody

eventually will, if you keep at it long enough and if you believe in yourself.

Barbara Alexander
Media Artists Group
Los Angeles

Luck is a component of success. And don't say, "Oh, gee, I've never been lucky." In poker, nobody gets all the winning hands. The trick is to minimize the bad cards and maximize the good ones. In order to do that, you have to know how to play the cards that are dealt to you.

What Can You Do For Yourself?

Over the years, we've started people from short films, from low-budget films, from commercials, from student films. You never know where the break is going to come. It depends on the person, about how much net-working the director can do, in the context of what the director can do for himself. He can't just sit back and expect the agent to do it. They almost have to get that initial break themselves. It's not that you can't work together, it's collaborative, but you've got to find somebody out there, ultimately that you build a rela-tionship with that says, "Hey, I really want to help you get started."

Marty Shapiro
Shapiro-Lichtman, Inc.
Los Angeles

Agents have many clients. Some are more success-ful than others. The agent is the same. She doesn't work differently for one client than another. It's the client and what they do; director or producer or anything. It's a matter of going after what you want. Directors have to be focused on what they want. Whether it is motion pictures or television. But they also have to follow up leads and call me up and say, "I heard about so and so, send them my reel." Or if I call them and say, "I'm down to two reels of film," don't tell me, "Well, I can't get it" or "I can't get there." They have to give me the ammunition.

Michele Wallerstein
Wallerstein Kappleman
Los Angeles

I think any good working relationship between a client and an agent is a team effort. They are in the marketplace. I am in the marketplace. They're hearing about things. I'm hearing about things. They hear about a situation, they call me, I go in and check it out.

Michael Douroux
Douroux & Co.
Los Angeles

New directors are sometimes so caught up in a visual style, they lose sight that they are there to work with (hopefully) a very talented bunch of performers and they have to make them feel good or they are not going to get a performance.

Rima Greer
Above the Line Agency
Los Angeles

My perspective of what the business is about is perception. What you want is to build a perception around a client that will give that client some heat and hopefully they'll have the talent to back it up . Most agents look to do that very quickly. I think it should be done over the period of time it takes to establish a strong foundation. Some people are in it for immediate money gratification and they tend to burn out because they haven't really

learned their craft.
Elliot Webb
Broder.Kurland.Webb.Uffner
Los Angeles

Our clients stay here for two reasons. The first reason is that we do a pretty good job. The second reason is that we need them to stay here. We derive our living from these people and we're trying to do a good job with the people we have. We feel the most effective way to get new clients is to do a good job for the people we already have. We only see people by referral. I am not in the volume business. I don't have 12 sub-agents.
Bob Hohman
Richland/Wunsch/Hohman
Los Angeles

I don't think there's anybody in the business who doesn't give everybody the benefit of however they want to define themselves. But, then you have to do it. If you keep saying you're a director and people keep running into you retailing clothes at Rick Pallick on weekends, pretty soon people say, "Wait a minute. Is this guy a haberdasher or is he a director?"
Gary Salt
Paul Kohner, Inc.
Los Angeles

A trait in common with a lot of people who don't make it is that they are self-destructive. There's not a real defining trait among people who do make it other than a real determination to make it.
Marty Shapiro
Shapiro-Lichtman
Los Angeles

Out of all the research I have done for varying books on the industry, the one thing that keeps impressing me is that those who win are very, very smart. Beverly Anderson, who is a New York talent agent put it very well:

■ *Be smart. Don't be naive. If you're not smart, it doesn't make any difference how much talent you have or how beautiful you are. You're dead. In all my experience of 29 years, all the people that I can sit here and say, made it or did not make it, did not make it because they were the most talented or the most beautiful or even the best organized or the most driven. They made it because basically, they were extremely smart human beings. It has nothing to do with the best looks and the best talent, the best voice or the best tap dancing ability. It's being smart. Donna Mills is smart. Alan Alda is smart. Johnny Carson is smart. Barbara Walters is smart. They made it because they're smart. Not because of talent. Talent is just automatic in this business.*

Who's to say that Barbra Streisand has the best voice in the world? I mean, let's face it, she sings well and has gorgeous styling and she makes a great sound, but who's to say if she has the best voice? I think the one ingredient that counts the most in this business is smarts. You could be talented and be sucked in by some agent who signs you up and never sends you out and you sit there for five years and say, "Well, I thought they were going to get me a job." Is that smart?" They promised they'd do a movie for me next year." To be smart is the best thing. Talent is like a dime a dozen out the window.

Beverly Anderson
Beverly Anderson Agency
New York

Here's what unit production manager Jack

Bohrer said about his friend Roger Corman:

Roger and I were classmates. He just breezed through with an incredible memory, great precision in his sciences and tremendous concentration. I worked with Roger on a number of his early films as assistant director and I'd have to get information from him to the rest of the crew between shots. I'd see him concentrating on the next scenes in the script and have to tap him on the shoulder four or five times—practically shake him—to get his attention. His mental focus was amazing. He was great at solving problems. It was a game to him, whether it was for physics or chemistry equations or reacting in a split second to a curve thrown his way about the lights or cameras on location.

> *How I Made a Hundred Movies in Hollywood and Never Lost a Dime*
> Roger Corman/Jim Jerome
> Dell Press, 1991

No one gets to be a star director or president of IBM without intense determination to make it. Not everyone needs to be a star and it is a trap to trivialize your accomplishments just because you are not yet visible and/or powerful. Just being one of the 5-10% in the Directors Guild who works regularly is a very large accomplishment.

Although famous names like Garry Marshall, Martha Coolidge, Hal Prince or Ron Link appear to be role models representing the success that we would all like to have, they're only more famous than many other directors with power, prestige and money whose names are unknown except to inveterate credit readers. These directors have achieved their goals and are making a living doing what they want to do. Not many people in the world get to do that.

Inspiration

My all time favorite inspirational quote comes from
Jim Carrey, star of *The Mask* and *Ace Ventura: Pet
Detective*. He knocked around Hollywood for at least
11 years before he began to be a *visible entity*.

I look at stuff that's happened in my life like it's
The Grapes of Wrath. *You know, you'll always win in
the end if you don't let the problems make you angry. I've
been through some wild times. When my father lost his job
and I was 13, we went from lower-middle class to complete poverty, living in a Volkswagen camper. My father
was not good at business because he was too nice. I learned
from that, not to be too nice when it comes down to the
crunch. I definitely have an edge because of all that. But
nothing made me go "Life sucks. People suck."*
    *I've always believed in magic. When I wasn't
doing anything in this town, I'd go up every night, sit on
Mulholland Drive, look out at the city, stretch out my
arms and say, "Everybody wants to work with me. I'm a
really good actor. I have all kinds of great movie offers."
I'd just repeat these things over and over, literally
convincing myself that I had a couple of movies lined up.
I'd drive down that hill, ready to take the world on, going,
"Movie offers are out there for me. I just don't hear them
yet." It was like total affirmations, antidotes to the stuff
that stems from my family background, from knowing
how things can go sour. Still, I've had times like that,
when I'd walk down the street, look at the street people
and feel like, "I'm already one of them. I'm already here."
I mean, I can scare the shit out of myself.*
    *Four years ago, I made a check for $10,000 to "Jim
Carrey, for acting services rendered." I put it in my wallet.
It's been there for four years. And, by Thanksgiving 1995,
guess what? I've already paid for my daughter's college*

*tuition and I bought a 1965 robins' egg blue T-bird
convertible, mint condition, and I'll be able to get a really
nice house. Nothing extravagant. See, I've always believed
that everything I've wanted, prayed for, will come to me
in one way or another. I'm real careful about what I ask
for. I asked God when I was young to give me whatever I
need to help me be a great actor-comedian. So, okay, it's
like now you're going to be poverty stricken, now you're
going to go through a divorce. I've always seen these things
as, "This rock is in my way for me to learn how to get
over." I expected to go on* Saturday Night Live, *do that
trip, but that didn't happen. But I got on* In Living
Color. *You may not always get where you expected but, so
long as you get somewhere, who cares?*

"Carrey'd Away"
Stephen Rebello
Movieline
July 1994

It's enlightening to consider some of the
synonyms the thesaurus lists for success: consum-
mation, prosperity, victory, triumph, fulfillment,
achievement, attainment, mastery. Just because you
haven't attained your ultimate fantasy, don't wait until
they are engraving your headstone to congratulate
yourself on how far you have come. I agree with
Michele Wallerstein:

*If you have talent and tenacity, you will make it.
If you have talent and you keep going back into the fray,
you will make it.*

Michele Wallerstein
Wallerstein Kappleman
Los Angeles

It is not wise to join any union until you are far
enough along to know that you have a strong
possibility of being hired for union work on a regular
basis. Even though being a member of the Directors
Guild of America or the Society of Stage Directors and
Choreographers is an authentic sign of validation by
the professional community, once you become a
member of the DGA, you violate the terms of
membership when you work for producers who have
not signed the DGA's collective bargaining agreement.
SSDC members must obtain special waivers to work
for other than their signatories.

    As a DGA member, you can no longer pick up
non-union work and add to your reel. Even though it
may seem that a union card is the key to admittance to
the 'private club' of working directors, if you had
access to the Guild's employment records, you would
note that vast numbers of directors holding cards are
just as unemployed as you, so take stock of where you
are in your career before you join. Sometimes a member may hire a non-member to do something he can't:

*I realized I needed some exteriors shot up in Big
Sur, which was* The Terror's *Baltic coastline. Since I was
a DGA member, I needed a non-union director. So I went
to my ace assistant, a young man I had hired months
earlier just out of the UCLA Film School. His name
was Francis Coppola... "Francis," I said, "this is your
chance. Go on up to Big Sur with Jack and Sandra and
shoot this stuff."*
    How I Made a Hundred Movies in
    Hollywood and Never Lost a Dime
    Roger Corman/Jim Jerome
    Dell Publishing, 1991

If you *are* far enough along in your career, membership is vital. Once you join, support your union. Scabbing hurts everyone.

The Directors Guild of America

The DGA represents directors, associate directors, stage managers and production associates. They forge and administer collective bargaining agreements, sponsor seminars, publish a membership directory and a bi-monthly magazine.

Admission to the DGA as a film director is based on obtaining employment by a production company that has signed the collective bargaining agreement (rules covering minimum salaries, working conditions, hours, residuals, etc.) with the Directors Guild. That company notifies the Guild via a deal memo of your impending employment. The Guild sends you the forms. You pay the one time only initiation fee of $6,500. Yearly dues are $50 per quarter plus 1.5% of your earnings over $10,000.

Television minimums vary relative to the length of the show. Primetime fees for ½ hours are $14,337, 1-hour shows are $24,347 with graduated increments up to $68,170 for 2 hours. Feature film fees vary from low- budget at $5,951 weekly to high-budget films over $500,000 at $9,469 weekly. Specials, non-prime-time, game shows, strip, variety, etc., all have special pay categories. Fees also include guarantees for number of weeks worked on specific types of projects.

Society of Stage Directors and Choreographers

The SSDC is the national independent labor union representing directors and choreographers who work in the American professional theater. The union has jurisdiction over Broadway, Off-Broadway, the League of Resident Theaters (LORT), Council of Stock Theaters (COST), Council of Resident Stock Theaters (CORST), the Indoor and Outdoor Musical Stock Theaters and the America Dinner Theater Institute (ADTI). These producers have recognized the Society as the exclusive representative for all directors and choreographers employed by them for the purpose of collective bargaining and the administration of matters within the scope of their agreements with SSDC.

Directors and Choreographers who work for these producers are immediately eligible to join SSDC. If you have not worked under one of the afore-mentioned agreements, but have directed and/or choreographed at least two Actors' Equity approved productions, you are eligible to join the Society.

Within these agreements, the union provides protection against labor abuses, services, collective bargaining agreements, arbitration, health insurance and a pension plan. They also publish a membership directory, a monthly Newsletter and a bi-annual Journal. SSD&C sponsors seminars, gives advice on minimum basic agreements and provides legal support.

The initiation fee is $1,000 with annual dues of $125 and fee assessments of 2.5% plus assessments of 2.5% of all royalties, up to a maximum annual assessment of $5,000 per company.

The Importance of Unions

Once you become a member of the unions, if you are at all active in your guild, you will realize the value of union membership for a number of reasons other than the vital forging of collective bargaining agreements and their enforcement. They provide seminars, support groups and workshops, not to mention the all-important pension and health benefits.

Since the industry is so overpopulated with those eager to work, it is always a mystery to me how unions were formed in the first place. There are always people who would be happy to work for less, with less prep time, for no health insurance and pension, without adequate safety precautions and without any of the safeguards that the union has fought for and won. A union is only as strong as its weakest link. Every time a member works for a production company that is not a signatory, he undermines the environment for everyone in the community, no matter which union he belongs to. It's essential to take your union seriously.

Directors Guild of America West 7920 Sunset Blvd. Los Angeles, CA 90046 310-289-2000	Directors Guild of America 520 N Michigan Ave. Chicago, IL 60611 312-644-5050
Directors Guild of America 110 W 57th St. New York, NY 10019 212-581-0370	Directors Guild of Great Britain 56 Whitfield Street London Wl England 71-880-9582

Society of Stage Directors & Choreographers P. O. Box 93847 Hollywood, CA 90093 310-854-6656
Society of Stage Directors & Choreographers 1501 Broadway, 31st floor New York, NY 10036-5653 212-391-1070/fax 212-302-6195

Wrap Up

Comfort and Wisdom
people who make it are focused
directors need patience
luck is a big component
positive thinking works
you don't have to be Spielberg to be successful

Union Membership
don't join until you are ready
provides emotional support
forges and enforces collective bargaining agreements
provides legal support
maintains pension and health benefits
sponsors workshops and support groups
don't take it for granted

11   Researching the Agents

There are various categories of agencies; big, small,
conglomerate, beginning, aggressive and/or just getting
by. Since agency/client relationships are so personal,
any classifications I might make would only be
subjective, so I'm presenting you the facts as best I can,
based upon my research and personal experience both
in interviewing these agents and my years in the
business.

There are new agencies with terrific agents
building their lists who, like you, will be the stars of
tomorrow. You could become a star with the right one
man/woman office and you could die on the vine at
CAA. There are no guarantees, no matter whom you
choose. The most important office in town might sign
you even without your union card, if your reel and/or
resume excites them. But mostly, they want you when
you are further along. Whomever you choose, if you
are to have a career of longevity, you can never
surrender your own vigilance in the process of your
career.

If you read carefully, you will be able to make
a wise decision using client lists, the agents' own
words, and the listing of each agency. It's unwise to
write off anybody. In this business, you just don't
know. One's own tastes and needs color the picture. I
could have an agent I love and you might hate him.

There are nice agents who are good agents and
there are nice agents who are bad agents. There are
agents who are not nice who are good agents and so
on. Just because I may think some agent is a jerk
doesn't mean he is. And even if he is, that might make
him a good agent, who knows? If I report it, no matter
how I write it, it always ends up looking petty.

If you read all the listings, you will have an

overview. If I think someone is *full of it*, read carefully, you'll figure it out. I've endeavored to present the facts plus whatever might have struck me about the agent; this one is a pilot and that one is a computer freak.

Some agents have survived for years without ever really *representing* their clients. They wait for the phone to ring. Some agents talk a better game than they play. I believe it is better to have no agent than an agent who is going to lie to you.

We all know the stereotypes about agents, "They lie, that's their job." Well, some agents lie, but most agents don't. Most agents are hard working, professional regular people who (like you) want to make it in show business. They too, want to be respected for their work, go to the Academy Awards and get great tables at Spago. And they, like you, are willing to put up with the toughest, most heartbreaking business in the world because they are mavericks who love the adventure and can't think of a single thing that interests them more.

I know many who read this book are just starting out and will be scanning the list for people who seem to be building their lists. There are many of those agents who have great potential. There are some who don't.

Other than CAA, ICM and WMA, I interviewed every agency personally to get their history. UTA didn't give me a personal interview, but I did speak to a spokesperson on the phone who gave me some information. Most of the time, I went to the office because that was the most convenient for the agent and seeing the office helped me make judgments about the agency. I didn't always meet everyone in every agency or all the partners, but I did meet with a partner or an agent who was acting as a spokesman for the company. I could be wrong in my judgments, but at least they are not based on hearsay.

I went through a real crisis about whom to include. Anybody who would talk to me? Only those agents that I could actually in good conscience recommend? It seems inappropriate for me to try to play God about who is worthy and who is not. On the other hand, I don't want my readers to think I would recommend everyone who is in the book. That automatically makes anyone not in the book suspect.

Also, there are people who for whatever reason won't talk to me. And I'm not talking about Mike Ovitz. I didn't even try to call him. What am I going to ask someone like Ovitz?" Gee, tell me, Mike. What's the best way for Oliver Stone to talk to you if he's not working?"

Shall I ask him the best way to keep in touch with him, if I am his client? I have no idea what it is like to exist in that area of the business. I am confident, however, that someone reading this book right now is embarked upon a journey that will arrive there. And if I am helpful to you in any way, I'll be expecting a call from you when you get there to fill me in on this particular information.

Agents reflect a major portion of the business. If you are currently employed in the business in any conspicuous way, people are usually nice to you and validate your existence. If you are not, the lack of respect is appalling. Keep your wits about you and you'll gain perspective when these same people fawn all over you once you actually do some visible work. Maybe their fawning is not just an exercise in fakery. It is true that successful people are usually sending off better vibes, although some are still stinkers. Whether you're gainfully employed in the business or not, endeavor to keep your sense of humor handy. What else can you do?

Some agents would not let me name any of their clients and others didn't mind if I named clients, they just didn't want to be responsible for singling any one out. As a whole, just assume that I looked up the client list plus credits and listed a few that I thought were representative of the list.

If you find an agency that seems to appeal to you, check the index in the back of the book to see if that agent has any quotes and if so, check them out, this will give you more insight.

When you query agents, be discriminating. Don't blanket the town with letters. Target the agent that seems right for you and ration yourself. It's a better use of your energy and more likely to pay off.

Agents are already inundated with reels and resumes, and while they are all looking for the next hot director, there are only so many hours in a day, so don't waste their time or yours. If you are just starting, don't expect CAA to come knocking at your door. Choose someone who is at the same level as you are and grow together.

If you have just gotten a job on your own, you will probably have some referrals already. Check them out and see who appeals to you. A job is not automatic entree. As you have probably noted throughout the book, most agents are not interested in a one shot deal. In my experience researching agents for directors, writers and actors, I keep learning again and again that agents are interested in a body of work. They want to see a progression of you and your product. They want to know that they are not squandering their hard won contacts on someone who doesn't have the ability to go the distance. They won't be able to buy a cottage in the south of France on their commissions for one job. Neither will you.

Like attracts like. You will ultimately get just what you want in an agent. I believe you can get a terrific agent. I believe you can be a terrific client. There are no shortcuts. And today is not the last day of your life. In her book, *My Lives*, Roseanne quotes a line from Sun Tzu's, *The Art of War*, which she says everyone in Hollywood has read. It says: "The one who cares most wins."

Good luck on your choices and remember me kindly. An actress is always looking for a good part.

Again: Check all addresses before mailing. Every effort has been made to provide accurate and current addresses and phone numbers, but agents move and computers goof. Call the office and verify the address. They won't know it's you.

⬛ Remember

✓ Your first agent is yourself. You must be your own agent until you attract someone who will care and has more access than you. It's better to keep on being your own agent than to have an agent without access or passion.

✓ Make yourself read all the listings before you make a decision. Then, cull your list down to five. If none of the five are interested, then you can go back and choose some more. If you find an agent who interests you, look in the index and see if he is quoted. If he is, this will give you more information.

✓ Mass mailings are usually a waste of money. There is no use sending CAA or ICM your reel without entree. It's pointless to query someone you have never heard of. If you have no information about the agent, how do you know you want him? Be selective.

✓ Don't blow your chances of being taken seriously by pursuing an agent before you are ready.

✓ Although they are called literary agents, in show business, that usually means they handle both writers *and* directors.

✓ Getting the right agent is not the answer to all your prayers—but, it's a start!

▐ Above the Line Agency

9200 Sunset Boulevard #401
just W of Doheny
Los Angeles, CA 90069
310-859-6115

On September 1, 1994, Rima Greer pulled off a tremendous achievement. She not only opened her own literary office representing writers, directors and a few actors, but she managed to leave her mentor/boss Joan Scott at Writers & Artists in a good mood.

Greer was a secretary for the Writers Guild before moving to William Morris and then to Writers & Artists for 12 years, ultimately as president of the literary department.

Rima's one woman office (with two assistants) will represent 12 writers and directors, and one actor. Clients include Monte Merrick, Gregory Widen, Greg Taylor, Jim Strain, Rama Stagner, John Hopkins, Ryan Rowe and Irvin Kershner.

She's not taking on anyone new for the present, preferring to concentrate on her current clients and her new business. You'll see quotes from Rima throughout the book. I like her a lot.

Agents
Rima Greer
Client List
12 directors
Clients
Irvin Kershner, Ryan Rowe, John Hopkins and others.

Bret Adams

448 W 44th Street
btwn 9th & 10th Avenues
New York, NY 10036
212-765-5630

Bret Adams has been an actor, a publicist, a producer, a manager of ACT, and a binocular renter at the theater. If it's in the theater, Bret probably did it. The number of things that Bret has managed to figure out a way to make money from in the business is a testimony to his creativity.

He started his own agency in 1971 and Mary Hardin has been his partner since 1982. Mary's original credentials came as a by product of being a dutiful wife to husband, director Richard Hardin. The gypsy life of a regional theater director requires moving every six months and since Mary went along doing whatever theater jobs were available, as Richard's resume grew, so did Mary's contacts. They now serve her well as an agent. The agency represents actors, writers, directors, conductors, set designers, costume and lighting designers, as well as directors for the opera. Clients from Bret's list of directors include Susan H. Schulman, John Going and Phil McKinley. A complete agency representing the theater, Bret and Mary are two of the most respected agents in the business.

Agents
Bret Adams and Mary Hardin.
Client List
20 writers and directors.
Clients
Susan H. Schulman, John Going, Phil McKinley, Jonathan Eaton, Worth Gardner and others.

◼ The Agency

1800 Avenue of the Stars
in Century City
Los Angeles, CA 90067
310-551-3000

Laurence S. Becsey and Richard C. Berman bought the
William Schuller Agency from their partner, William
Schuller, in the 1970s renaming it Talent Management
International. When TMI merged with WMA/MCA
agent and packaging pioneer, Jerome Zeitman, the new
name was The Agency. Zeitman's background also
included producing for Wolper Productions and
Columbia Pictures.

Berman and Becsey are now gone (Becsey has a
new agency, Becsey.Wisdom.Kalajian) and Zeitman is
the sole owner of The Agency.

Emile Gladstone, who heads up the crew
representing directors, was at ITC Entertainment
before he joined The Agency. Colleagues on the
directors team include Nick Mechanic, who became an
agent at The Agency, Harvard MBA Walter Morgan
(from Business Affairs at Fox), Walter Van Dyke from
Triad and owner, Zeitman.

Agents
Emile Gladstone, Jerry Zeitman, Walter Van Dyke,
Walter Morgan and Nick Mechanic.
Client List
15 directors
Clients
Steve Cornwell, Ivan Passer, Clair Foster and others.

APA/Agency for the Performing Arts

9000 Sunset Boulevard #900
E of Doheny
Los Angeles, CA 90069
310-273-0744

The past two years have marked a time of great change
for APA. The deaths of beloved president Marty Klein
and powerful John Gaines plus the departure of Tom
Korman and Larry Masser left a void in leadership at
the most personal conglomerate in town. APA began
to energize itself as the new *young turks* took over, led
by senior vice-president Steve Tellez. Then CAA stole
Steve away and APA had to regroup again.

Katy Rothacker from the New York office
replaces Steve as the agency finds itself on the upswing.
Rothaker headed The William Morris Agency's casting
department from 1988-1992. David Kalodner just
returned to the company after a year as an independent
film producer.

Long known as the place for comedy
development, APA continues to hold top honors in
this department. Danny Robinson heads that division
and his comedy development showcases held two to
three times a year are hot tickets with studio, network
and casting executives. Danny's speciality is spotting
emerging comics and bringing them to the attention of
the rest of the staff.

People keep saying APA is down for the count,
but APA is still the only full-service (writers, producers, actors and directors, books, plays, personal
appearance, music, concerts, college tours, etc.) alterna-
ive to the mega-agencies. If you want some kind of
personal attention (they only have 250 clients

▚ APA/Agency for the Performing Arts

888 Seventh Avenue
at 59th Street
New York, NY 10016
212-582-1500

worldwide), then APA may be a viable choice for you.
Still connected enough to get you in, the staff/client
ratio gives you a much better chance for personal
attention to career development than any of the other
conglomerates.

Because they need to try harder, APA does.
They develop talent, check out the town and return
phone calls.

In Los Angeles, television directors are handled
by Lee Dintsman and feature directors are represented
by David Saunders. The New York office handles very
few directors for the theater. Ana Maria Alessi heads
the literary department in New York.

Agents
Los Angeles: Lee Dinstman and David Saunders.
New York: Anna Maria Alessi.
Client List
250 all clients
Clients
Roy Campanella, Jr., Noel Nosseck, Paul Shapiro,
Oley Sassoni, Victoria Hochberg and others.

■ The Artists Agency

10000 Santa Monica Boulevard # 305
at Century Park East
Los Angeles, CA 90067
310-277-7779

Sandy Bresler left ICM in 1971 to create an elegant,
smaller, more personal agency named The Sandy
Bresler Agency. When he was joined by ICM expat-
riates Jim Cota, Mike Livingston and Don Wolff, the
name became Bresler, Wolff, Cota, and Livingston. In
1980 the current name was adopted. In 1984, Sandy left
to start his own agency once again.

The current partners are the above mentioned
founders plus Mickey Freiberg and Dick Shepherd.
Jimmy Cota is gracious enough to still speak to me
even though he said the onslaught of mail he received
from *The LA Agent Book* was somewhat more than he
might have wanted to handle. With this in mind, *please*
do not send your reel or resume to this agency (or any
other) without sending a query letter *first*. The
material won't be viewed and may or may not be
returned. Directing clients of this agency are serviced
by partners Mickey Freiberg, Richard Shepherd,
Jimmy Cota, Merrily Kane and Andy Patman.

Agents
Mickey Freiberg, Dick Shepherd, Andy Patman,
Jimmy Cota and Merrily Kane.
Client List
100 writers and directors.
Clients
Michael Peters, Edward James Olmos and others.

▇ The Artists Group

1930 Century Park West #403
S of Santa Monica Boulevard
Los Angeles, CA 90067
310-552-1100

The founder of The Artists Group, Arnold Soloway,
(Susan Smith Associates, Kumen-Olenick) has now left
the agency he started in 1975. His company is now in
the hands of partners Hal Stalmaster and Robert
Malcolm. Hal and Robert (who travels back and forth
between the LA and NY offices) have continued to
build the office past the point of actors to include
directors, writers, producers, technicians, below-the-
line personnel and packaging.

Art Rutter, who shepherds the literary clients,
has a diverse background: he started his career working
as a production administrator on ABC Television's
now defunct soap opera, *Ryan's Hope*, was a network
executive at ABC Entertainment, an agent trainee at
William Morris, a talent agent at The Agency and
helped form the Literary Department at Harry Gold
and Associates. He was brought to The Artists Group
in 1991 to give more form to the department
representing writers and directors. Prior to that time,
although the agency represented writers, directors,
producers and below-the-line personnel, there was no
formal literary department as such. Today, Art
oversees that department's affairs, although Susan
Grant and Hal Stalmaster both have their own lists of
directors.

Director clients include Marcus Cole, David
Blyth and Massimo Massocco. Best to come to this
agency through referral.

The Artists Group East

1650 Broadway #711
at 52nd Street
New York, NY 10019
212-586-1452

Agents
Art Rutter, Susan Grant and Hal Stalmaster.
Client List
15-20 directors.
Clients
Marcus Cole, David Blyth, Massimo Massocco
and others.

▣ BDP & Associates

10637 Burbank Boulevard
1 block W of Cahuenga
North Hollywood, CA 91601
818-506-7615

Sharon Debord started out as a secretary at this agency
and now owns the business. The initials stand for
Sharon and former partners Walter Beakel and Morgan
Paull who have since left the business. Paull is
recovering from the business by sailing his boat around
the world.

Since the agency was created 10 years ago, it
has continued to grow and prosper.

Debord mainly services actors, but does list one
director on her list. She certainly won't be able to tell
you her list is overcrowded. Sharon handles soap
director Ken Herman.

Agents
Sharon Debord
Client List
1 director.
Clients
Ken Herman

▰ The Brandt Co.

12700 Ventura Boulevard #340
just E of Coldwater
across from Jerry's Deli
Studio City, CA 91604
818-506-7747

Geoffrey Brandt manages as a sole proprietor with the powerful client list of a large conglomerate. One of my favorite directors, Lamont Johnson (*Last Great American Hero, My Sweet Charlie, The Execution of Private Slovak*, etc.), has been his client for years.

From a show biz family (relatives founded The American Film Institute, the National Association of Theater Owners, the Brandt Theaters, etc.) Geoffrey must have found it just a hop, skip and a jump from working as the Associate Artistic Director of the New Jersey Shakespeare Festival to being a talent agent at William Morris and creating the directors' division at APA. In 1989, Brandt formed this company with a very small list of important writers, directors, editors, costume designers and producers.

A charming and articulate man, Geoffrey displays humanity, taste, class and clout.

Agents
Geoffrey Brandt
Client List
22 clients.
Clients
Michael Backes, Stuart Birnbaum, Doug Borgi, Lamont Johnson and others.

■ Becsey · Wisdom · Kalajian

9229 Sunset Boulevard #710
W of Doheny
Los Angeles, CA 90069
310-550-0535

Laurence Becsey managed to take his law degree, skip
the mailroom and start as an agent at WMA 22 years
ago. Along the way, Becsey and partner Richard
Berman bought The William Schuller Agency and
changed the name to Talent Management International. When they merged with Jerry Zeitman in the
'80s, the name became The Agency. In 1990, Becsey
left to open the Laurence S. Becsey Agency where he
was joined by colleagues Victoria Wisdom (ICM, Tom
Chasin) and Jerry Kalajian (APA).

In 1993, when Wisdom and Kalajian became
partners, their names joined the masthead. BWK
represents a list of 50 directors, writers and producers
about 20 of whom are directors. Tom Holland (*The
Langoliers*), Jeremy Kagan (*Journey of Natty Gunn*) and
Ken Cameron (*Oldest Living Confederate Tells All*) are
names from their impressive list. Not for beginners,
BWK reads query letters, but accepts no unsolicited
material.

Agents
Laurence S. Becsey, Victoria Wisdom and
Jerry Kalajian.
Client List
20 directors.
Clients
Tom Holland, Jeremy Kagan, Kevin Connor, Ken
Cameron, Cynthia Scott, Brian Singer and others.

Broder·Kurland··Webb·Uffner

9242 Beverly Boulevard # 200
at Maple Drive
Beverly Hills, CA 90210
310-281-3400

Gazing at the waiting room walls at the Broder·
Kurland·Webb·Uffner Agency which are covered with
Directors Guild Awards and Emmy citations for
people like Donald Bellisario (*Quantum Leap*), James
Burrows (*Cheers*) and Les Charles and Glen Charles
(creators of *Cheers*), I'm hard put to think of anyone
with a more impressive list of writers and directors,
editors, cinematographers, costume designers and
authors. Clearly at the top of the list, BKWU is an
agency to aspire to.

Bob Broder was an agent at IFA, and Norman
Kurland worked for Leonard Hanzer (Major Talent)
before they decided to join forces to represent writers
and directors in 1978 (Broder Kurland). I interviewed
the third partner to join the operation, Elliot Webb.
Webb's degrees are in marketing and finance. In 1972,
his first job was finding employment for high-priced
accounting and financial personnel, but it was his
venture selling sweatshirts at Madison Square Garden
that Webb managed to parlay into becoming an agent.
Because he had to negotiate a contract with The
William Morris Agency (who represented a sports-
caster), he became aware for the first time of agenting
as a profession. That information led him to WMA
University in the mailroom.

Creative enough to circumvent actually
delivering mail (he drove executives to the airport),
Elliot became secretary to various agents at the

---

renowned agency. As Elliot describes it, "I was the secretary to the agent who handled the horse, Secretariat. My career was nowhere," when he left for California with an entree to IFA. IFA soon merged with CMA to form ICM, where Elliot spent 10 years, eventually running the television literary department. Webb's partners, Kurland and Broder, had been urging Webb to join their partnership for years before he finally succumbed in 1983. Former ICM colleague Beth Uffner was not only head of development at MTM, but ran her own successful agency before becoming the fourth partner in 1989.

Elliot is happy to point out that although most of their clients have been with them for many years, the life blood of the agency is acquiring new young talent. Although they look at query letters, the main avenue for new people is referrals from some-one already in the business, so be creative and find someone connected to this agency before querying.

Agents
Elliot Webb, Beth Uffner, Bob Broder, Norman Kurland, Joel Milner, Rhonda Gomez-Quinones, Bruce Kaufman, Ian Greenstein, Tammy Stockfish and Gayla Nethercott.
Client List
Large.
Clients
Check Director Guild Membership Directory.

▀ Don Buchwald & Associates

9229 Sunset Boulevard # 710
W of Doheny
Los Angeles, CA 90069
310-278-3600

Years ago, Don Buchwald was one of my first agents in
New York at the commercial powerhouse agency,
Abrams-Rubaloff. He had his own exclusive theatrical
agency before joining A-R and has now combined his
earlier theatrical interests with his commercial assets to
produce the powerful agency he runs today.

In 1992, Renee Jennett (APA, Strain Jennett)
left the New York office to help Don open the West
Coast office. The Los Angeles office focuses on theater,
film and television representation for actors, writers,
producers and directors.

My memories of Don are vivid as a strong
negotiator who knows the business. He's adept at
knowing when to be tough and when to be flexible.

Buchwald's list of directors is select and
presided over by Tim McNeil. New York directing
clients are represented by Traci Ching.

Don Buchwald & Associates

10 E 44th Street
just E of 5th Avenue
New York, NY 10017
212-867-1200

Agents
Los Angeles: Tim McNeil
New York: Traci Ching
Client List
12 directors.
Clients
Paul Lazurus, Sheldon Epps and others.

Contemporary Artists

1427 Third Street Promenade, Suite 205
at Broadway
Santa Monica, CA 90401
310-395-1800

After the demise of MCA in 1963, Ron Leif opened his own office. Known at one time as Contemporary Korman, this prestigious agency has an important list of writers, directors, producers and actors.

Contemporary Artists is respected and has access. Directing clients at this company include Chris Pechin and Michael Preece. Bill Hart represents directors at this agency.

Agents
Bill Hart
Client List
Check DGA listings.
Clients
Chris Pechin, Michael Preece and others.

▦ The Cooper Agency

10100 Santa Monica Boulevard #310
in Century City
Los Angeles, CA 90067
310-277-8422

Frank Cooper was secretary to the *real* William Morris
in New York during the early years of the depression.
Morris asked Frank why he was studying accounting
when he could focus his sights on what was going to
become "an interesting business." When Morris died,
Frank took Morris' advice and started his own agency
representing talent. At one point, he worked for what
is now ICM and at other times, he not only had his
own agency, but was a pioneer in what is now known
as packaging; marrying writers, talent and producers.
He was Frank Sinatra's first agent, as well as Dinah
Shore's. He found Alan Young and a writer and sold
what became the hit series, *Mr. Ed* to Bristol Myers. By
1964, Cooper had an agency that represented over 500
writers, producers, directors, entertainers and actors.
With so many important clients all over the world,
Cooper spent two weeks out of four on an airplane
and it all became too much. He sold his agency to
Ashley-Famous and, though he stayed on with his
clients, he wasn't happy.

Finally, he quit show business. After a week,
old clients were on his phone night and day for
guidance. Finally, his wife said, "You need an office if
you are going to do this."

Still going strong, The Cooper Agency is not
kidding around. There are two generations of Coopers
representing the 50 or so high profile clients on the list.
Frank's son, Jeff, has been associated with his dad for

27 years.

The Cooper Agency represents writers, producers, directors, composers, lyricists and authors.

Agents
Frank Cooper and Jeff Cooper.
Client List
3 directors.
Clients
Robert Scheerer, Nick Havinga and Fred Gallo.

■ CAA/Creative Artists Agency

9830 Wilshire Boulevard
at Little Santa Monica
Beverly Hills, CA 90212-1825
310-288-4545

Much has been written about the power, prestige and
inscrutability of Creative Artists Agency. Many people
are heard to say that instead of the big three, which
used to mean CAA, ICM and WMA, there is now
really the big *one* and that the one is CAA. With the
inroads ICM has made this year, the distance has
narrowed considerably, but Mike Ovitz is still the
number one power broker in town. Instrumental in
the buyout of Universal Studios by Matsushita, Ovitz
was seen to be "pushing the envelope" until his foray as
consultant to France's Credit Lyonnais bank got
everyone's attention. Thought to be a conflict of
interest by his rivals and others, Ovitz drew fire from
all fronts. A little heat never bothers Ovitz and the
company continues to be the dominant force in the
entertainment business.

     The agency was founded in 1975 by Michael
Ovitz, Bill Haber, Rowland Perkins, Ron Meyer, and
Michael Rosenfield. When these dynamic men left
William Morris, they "...didn't have any clients. They
didn't have any financing. They didn't have any
offices. In fact, between the five of them, they only
had one car...They couldn't afford to hire a
receptionist. So each of their wives filled in one day a
week." ("CAA: Packaging of an Agency," by Charles
Schreger, *Los Angeles Times,* April 23, 1979).

     In 1990, the carless wonders moved into a
magnificent building designed by I. M. Pei. As students

of Japanese management techniques, they teach fellow agents to suppress individual ego. This method of doing business has been credited with their success, but as Ovitz sees it, "CAA grew simply because it was better than others at helping the talent realize its ends." ("Inside the Agency", by Michael Cieply, Calendar, *Los Angeles Times*, July 2, 1989). CAA not only has 134 actor clients but also 288 writers, 146 directors, and Magic Johnson (according to the July 9, 1989, *The New York Times* article by L.J. Davis entitled "Hollywood's Most Secret Agent").

Clients include the cream of theater, film and television talent: Oliver Stone, Robert Zemeckis, Sydney Pollack, Steven Spielberg, Harold Becker, Alan W. Parker, Peter Bogdanovich, James Ivory and many, many others.

Lists of agents at the big agencies are guarded like Fort Knox, so other than the partners, my agent listings are tentative and based on the trades.

Agents
Mike Ovitz, Bill Haber, Ron Meyer, Rowland Perkins, Todd Smith, David O'Connor, David Tenzer, Michael Menchel, Adam Krentzman, Glenn Bickel, Sonya Rosenfield, Jack Rapke, Rand Holston, Jane Sindell, Rosalie Swedlin, David Lonner, Joe Rosenberg, Brian Lourd, Justin Connolly and some 60 others.
Client List
Very large.
Clients
Andrew Davis, Harold Ramis, Sydney Pollack, Steven Spielberg, Oliver Stone, Robert Zemeckis, Robert Redford, Peter Weir, Ivan Reitman, Gene Reynolds and many, many others.

DGRW/Douglas, Gorman, Rothacker & Wilhelm, Inc.

1501 Broadway #703
btwn 43rd & 44th Streets
New York, NY 10036
212-382-2000

Douglas, Gorman, Rothacker & Wilhelm, Inc. was
established in 1988 when Fred Gorman (Bret Adams)
joined Flo Rothacker (Ann Wright), Jim Wilhelm
(Lionel Larner, Eric Ross, The Barry Douglas Agency)
and Barry Douglas (ICM) to form a New York
miniconglomerate that is congenial and well-
connected.

Known primarily as a source for distinguished
actors, DGRW also handles directors, writers, choreographers and musical directors.

The 15 or so directing clients tended by
partners Gorman, Wilhelm and Douglas all have
handshake deals with the agency, although they sign
contracts from job to job. Since these are handshake
arrangements, I'm not listing clients' names.

Agents
Fred Gorman, Barry Douglas and Jim Wilhelm.
Client List
15 directors.
Clients
Hand-shake, so not listed with DGA or SSD&C.

■ The Directors Network

12401 Ventura Boulevard # C
at Rhodes, 1 block E of Whitsett
Studio City CA 91604
818-506-3696

The only agent I have in the book who specializes in
directors for commercials, Steve Lewis entered the
business as an editor of television commercials in 1961.
He edited segments, commercials and promos as well as
directed them before deciding to open his agency in
1985. His agency represents Los Angeles based
commercial directors and directors of photography for
regional commercial production companies throughout the country. His marketplace has now expanded
to buyers around the world, but mostly the US,
Canada and Mexico.

Steve represents very specialized directors to
production companies looking to fill a particular need.
Although most commercial directors were originally
on staff at production companies, Steve pioneered a
new concept in this part of the business. All his clients
are niche directors, specializing in action, kids,
dialogue, etc. His list goes "from C to A+ and they all
work in 35mm."

Although he does look at reels, they should be
no more than ten minutes and they should contain
clips and/or trailers of your work. If you have only
one piece of film, don't bother. You are not far enough
along. Steve's interest is immediately provoked if you
are from Pasadena's famous Art Design Center or a
graduate of a film school with many examples of your
work. Look at his quotes elsewhere for more specifics
on the reel and for his ideas on when you are ready.

Don't inundate the man with film if you are looking at commercials as an entree into features or television. He says it doesn't work that way.

The Directors Network has 20 directors and 20 Directors of Photography. Seventy percent of the list are director-cameramen.

Although client Lorraine Senna Ferrara has directed on *Home Front*, *Picket Fences* and *Northern Exposure*, Steve says this doesn't happen often and is still difficult because of scheduling.

His colleague, Susie Goldberg, was an AD and a producer of commercials. Bill Despoto became an agent at The Directors Network and works exclusively with Directors of Photography.

Although Steve's list is based in either New York or Los Angeles, he is open to unique talent no matter where, although he says it is easier if you live in one of those two large production centers. He's in the market for a great Latino director.

Agents
Steve Lewis, Susie Goldberg and Bill Despoto.
Client List
20 directors.
Clients
Bruce Logan, Barbara Kanowitz, Rob Thomas, Jan Peterson, Lorraine Senna Ferrara and others.

▰ Douroux & Co.

445 S Beverly Drive #310
4 blocks S of Wilshire
Beverly Hills, CA 90212
310-552-0900

In March of 1977, Michael Douroux escaped from IBM
and entered show business to work as an executive in
business affairs for Norman Lear. A Los Angeles native
and USC graduate, Michael always wanted to be
involved in the industry and when a chance meeting
produced a showbiz job offer, Michael took it.

When Stu Robinson and Bernie Weintraub
(Robinson Weintraub, now paradigm) offered Michael
a chance to add to his negotiating skills and business
affairs acumen and become a literary agent, it fulfilled
Michael's wish to become more creatively involved.

In 1983, Michael was ready to open his own
agency with partner Candace Lake. Lake & Douroux
lasted until 1991 when Michael founded Douroux &
Co. to represent directors and writers. An alternative
to conglomerate representation, Michael's idea is to
provide career management with very hands on in-
volvement. Booking jobs doesn't excite him; sculpt-
ing a career does. Michael has some very practical
quotes elsewhere. Be sure to check them out.

Agents
Michael E. Douroux plus one.
Client List
20+ directors.
Clients
Linda Day, Reynaldo Villalobos, Perry Lang,
Tom Straw and others.

Duva - Flack Associates, Inc.

200 W 57th Street #407
just W of 7th Avenue
New York, NY 10019
212-957-9600

Originally an actor, Robert Duva began pestering his
agent at Talent Associates to become her assistant
instead of her client. He became her colleague and then
worked with Mort Schwartz, Robby Lantz and The
Gersh Agency New York.

Elin Flack's show-biz baptism was as a
secretary for Lionel Larner. She became an agent at LL
and then worked for Don Buchwald and Robert
Abrams Associates before joining J. Michael Bloom in
1981.

Elin and Bob had known each other as
competitors for 15 years when a friend who knew that
each of them was pondering new paths suggested they
meet. Although both were skeptical, they meshed
immediately and in October of 1993, when other
agencies were merging or closing, these two tasteful,
connected agents decided to join forces representing
actors, writers, directors, director/choreographers,
designers and writers.

Even though their client list in every discipline
is stellar, they do still take the time to start young
artists or jump-start careers that are stalled.

Agents
Robert Duva and Elin Flack.
Clients
3 directors.
Client List
Nicholas Hytner, Lonny Price and Andre Ernotte.

Epstein/Wyckoff & Associates

280 S Beverly Drive # 400
S of Wilshire Boulevard
Beverly Hills, CA 90212
310-278-7222

Craig Wyckoff and Gary Epstein were both actors
before they each chose (for different reasons) to leave
acting and become agents. Craig decided that agenting
would be more challenging and proved it by joining
The William Felber Agency and developing the
television and film department. It wasn't long before
he had his own agency.

Gary, a New York actor who "became addicted
to eating and paying his rent," ran his own agency
(Phoenix Artists) before merging with Craig in 1991.

Directors at the agency are represented by
Karen Wakefield. She maintains a hands on
relationship with all her clients. Karen was an
independent producer and worked in development
with Dan Curtis before she decided to change sides of
the desk. She joined E/W in 1988, shepherding her list
of directors and writers as they become more and more
successful.

Partner Gary Epstein represents the handful of
New York theater directors on the list.

Epstein/Wyckoff & Associates

311 W 43rd Street
btwn 7th and 8th Avenues
New York, NY 10036
212-586-9110

Agents
Karen Wakefield (Los Angeles)
Gary Epstein (New York)
Client List
5-6 directors.
Clients
Check Directors Guild Membership Directory.

▦ Maggie Field Agency

12725 Ventura Boulevard # D
in Calico Corners shopping area
Studio City, CA 91604
818-980-2001

Although Maggie Field says she became an agent by
mistake, she has tracked a straight line from her first
job typing *Ironside* scripts in the steno pool at Universal, through secretary/assistant to a literary agent at
William Morris, on to a publishing company, assisted
another literary agent and finally becoming an agent at
Zeigler Ross. She worked at Writers & Artists as well
as Robinson Weintraub before burnout caused her to
leave the business in 1984. Batteries recharged, Maggie
decided to see what the other side of the desk was like,
joining Disney as a buyer. Horrified at the treatment
of writers and directors, she vowed to open her own
office representing and protecting writers and
directors.

Although Maggie's list is heavy with writers
and producers, the agency does represent a few directors, led by Judy Chech (Triad). Clients include Kris
Tabori, Phil Sgricca, James Darren, John McPherson
and Terrence O'Hara. Don't query this agency on
your own. Your only possible entree is through
someone who knows one of the agents there.

Agents
Maggie Field and Judy Chech.
Client List
35 writers and directors.
Clients
Kris Tabori, Phil Sgricca, James Darren,
John McPherson and Terrence O'Hara.

▣ The Gage Group

9255 Sunset Boulevard # 515
just W of Doheny
Los Angeles, CA 90069
310-859-8777

Former actor Martin Gage was hit by a cab on the way
back from his third callback for Baby John in the
original production of *West Side Story*. He must have
taken that as God's comment on his acting, because,
by the time I met Martin in 1968, he was working as
an agent in New York for Fifi Oscard. Fearless, a
brilliant agent and a crazy human being, Martin is
someone you can't help but like. He's got an eye for
talent and for agents.

Martin finds time to function as a guru for not
only the actors, but his directors and playwrights as
well. Literary department head Jonathan Westover was
an assistant, casting commercials at JHR. He then
interned at the prestigious Richland/Wunsch/Hohman
Agency before his arrival at GG as assistant to then
literary boss, Karen Bohrman. Jonathan and Martin are
joined by colleague Wanda Moore in repping the
directors. Moore was in development at independent
production companies, as well as Tristar. Directing
clients at this agency include Kenneth Frankel, Lipo
Ching and Jenny Sullivan.

Agents
Martin Gage, Jonathan Westover and Wanda Moore.
Client List
17 directors.
Clients
Kenneth Frankel, Lipo Ching, Jenny Sullivan and
others.

▣ The Gersh Agency

232 N Canon Drive
S of Little Santa Monica
Beverly Hills, CA 90210
310-274-6611

Phil Gersh has been part of the Hollywood scene since
the days when agents were not allowed past the studio
gates. A legend in the business, Phil opened The Gersh
Agency in the late '70s and it has become one of the
most important and prestigious independent agencies
in town with a glittering list of directors, actors,
writers and below-the-line personnel that quickly
command attention and respect.

Agents who represent the likes of Arthur
Hiller and Amy Heckerling as well as newcomers like
Matty Rich, Steve Anderson and Nadia Tass, are Phil,
his son David, Nancy Nigrosh, Maryann Kelly, Lee
Keele, Jim Lefkowitz and Richard Arlook.

Agents
Phil Gersh, David Gersh, Nancy Nigrosh,
Maryann Kelly, Lee Keele, Jim Lefkowitz and
Richard Arlook.
Client List
Large.
Clients
Jan DeBont, Arthur Hiller, Dennis Dugan, Amy
Heckerling, Matthew Patrick, Richard Benjamin,
Jeffrey Hayden, Ian Sander, George L. Schaefer, Dick
Richards , Abraham Polonsky, Geoffrey Sherman,
Matty Rich, Steve Anderson, Yurek Bogayavicz,
Ronny Yu, Gary Shimokawa and others.

The Gersh Agency New York

130 W 42nd Street #2400
btwn 5th & 6th Avenues
New York, NY 10036
212-997-1818

The Gersh Agency New York was formed in the mid-eighties when David Guc (pronounced Gus), Scott Yoselow (William Morris), Ellen Curren (The O'Neill Playwright's Foundation) and Mary Meagher left Don Buchwald & Associates to form the New York office of the prestigious Los Angeles firm Phil started so long ago. The bulk of the work of the literary department of this important agency is handled through the Los Angeles office. Even so, the New York office manages to be busy enough to enlist the efforts of four agents, so Los Angeles is obviously not doing all the business.

Mary Meagher left for WMA, but partner Scott Yoselow heads up the literary department. Susan Morris is the book agent and Jennifer Lyne handles below-the-line clients.

New clients in this agency are mostly seen by industry referral.

Agents
David Guc and Scott Yoselow.
Client List
220 (NY/LA) total clients.
Clients
Check Los Angeles listing (shared list)

Gold Marshak and Associates

3500 W Olive #1400
at Riverside
Burbank, CA 91505
818-972-4300

In 1981 Harry opened The Harry Gold Agency and asked Darryl Marshak to be his partner, and in 1992, Darryl accepted. If Harry is as persistent getting his clients jobs (and he is), then it's easy to see how this agency has continued to grow and succeed while others have fallen by the wayside. Harry (who was originally an actor) trained with The Robert Light Agency and Herb Tannen before opening his own office. While Harry was starting his business, Darryl continued to work with his mentor/boss Diane Davis at Twentieth Century Artists before joining Craig Wyckoff and forming Marshak/Wyckoff. An entrepreneur, Darryl was a student filmmaker, director, producer and the founder of the moving company called Starving Students before he went to work for Diane. In 1990, Darryl finally joined Harry and in late 1992, the partnership became official.

The literary department at Gold Marshak is headed by Jeff Melnick. After years as a studio exec at Universal, Columbia and Metromedia, Jeff opened his first agency in 1989 repping such talent as John Patrick Shanley (*Moonstruck*) and Rob Epstein and Jeff Friedman (*Common Threads*). He also worked for the noted literary office of Curtis Brown. Jeff proudly points out that every year at least one of his clients receives some industry accolade, whether it be an Oscar, Emmy or DGA award. Evan Corday, whose background includes Triad and Lorimar, is Jeff's

---

colleague. They have two directing clients.

Agent
Jeff Melnick and Evan Corday.
Client List
25 writers and directors.
Clients
Helaine Head and Nancy Malone.

▐ Innovative Artists

1999 Avenue of the Stars #2850
in Century City
Los Angeles, CA 90067
310-553-5200

The prestigious talent agency that Scott Harris and
Howard Goldberg created has transformed itself
significantly since 1982, when they opened the west
coast offices for Robert Abrams (Abrams Harris &
Goldberg). A glittering client list, coupled with major
agency additions like status literary agent, Frank
Wuliger, have resulted in even more dimension and
credibility. In 1991 when Wuliger arrived, the name
was changed to reflect the addition: Innovative Artists
Talent and Literary Agency.

Wuliger, who heads the literary department,
traveled the route of most important agents, beginning
in the mailroom at the William Morris Agency. He
assisted at a prestigious office before creating the
literary department at APA in 1980. Frank was a
senior executive in the motion picture department at
ICM before producing for two years with Walter
Mirisch. He was also an executive at DEG. Frank
returned to agenting at The Agency in 1986.

In addition to Frank, agents at IA who represent directors are Sandy Weinberg, whose previous
life included time spent as Bill Block's assistant
at ITA, plus a stint at prestigious old-line office, H. N.
Swanson and colleague James Ward.

▟ Innovative Artists

130 W 57th Street #5B
W of Avenue of the Americas
New York, NY 10019
212-315-4455

Innovative represents writers, directors, producers and below-the-line personnel. New clients usually come through industry referral. Query letters are discouraged, but always read. Do not query this agency unless you have entree.

Frank heads the impressive literary department of this agency and reps about 15-20 directors.

Though founder Howard Goldberg died in 1993, the agency continues his legacy.

Agents
Frank Wuliger, Sandy Weinberg and James Ward.
Client List
15-20 directors.
Clients
Joyce Chopra, Tommy Lee Wallace, Alister Reed and others.

ICM/International Creative Management

8942 Wilshire Boulevard
just W of Robertson
Beverly Hills, CA 90211
310-550-4000

Everyone far and wide knows that CAA (Creative Artists Agency) is absolutely the most powerful agency in the world. Or are they? In 1991, power shifted appreciably. ICM made inroads when important William Morris agents defected to ICM and brought significant clients (Julia Roberts, Tim Robbins, Angelica Huston, etc.) with them to join other big guns like Eddie Murphy and Arnold Schwarzenegger who were already in residence. Then, in the great agency shakeup of 1992, Bill Block (head of prestigious boutique InterTalent), disbanded his agency and returned to ICM as head of the West Coast office.

Headed by chairman Jeff Berg, mighty ICM is intent on replacing CAA as the number one talent agency in the world. When United Kingdom based booking agencies Fair Warning/ICM and Wasted Talent merged to become ICM International, even more luster was added to the ICM crown. Currently number two in the showbiz hierarchy, ICM is poised for combat.

Formed when Ashley-Famous and CMA merged in 1971, this agency has many, many clients and many, many agents. The most famous are powerful Sam Cohn, who heads the New York office and charismatic Los Angeles based, WMA grad, Ed Limato. Ed was profiled in a *Vanity Fair* article, "The Famous

ICM/International Creative Management

40 W 57th Street
W of 5th Avenue
New York, NY 10019
212-556-5600

Eddie L" in January 1990. If you have the credits to consider this agency, a trip to the library to read this article is a must.

Agents

Los Angeles: Alan Greenspan, Michael Black, Bill Douglas, Barbara Dreyfus, Richard Feldman, Diane Cairns, Mitch Douglas, Lee Gabler, Toni Howard, Scott Amovitz, Steve Rabineau, Joe Rosenberg, Scott Schwartz, Jim Wiatt, David Lonner, Bob Gumer, Dave Wirtschafter, Alan Berger, Nancy Josephson, Jeff Berg, Lou Pitt and many others.
New York: Sam Cohn, Lisa Loosemore, Boaty Boatwright, Paul Martino, Andrea Eastman, Sue Leibman and many others.

Client List

Very large.

Clients

Bernardo Bertolucci, John Boorman, Karel Reisz, Peter P. Benchley, John Frankenheimer, Gene Saks, Woody Allen, Garry Marshall, John Hancock, Randal Kleiser, Michael Mann, Mike Nichols, Bob Rafelson, Michael Ritchie, John Schlesinger and many others.

◼️🎬 Kaplan Stahler Agency

8383 Wilshire Boulevard #923
at San Vicente Boulevard
Beverly Hills, CA 90211
213-653-4483

Mitch Kaplan and Elliot Stahler graduated from The William Morris Agency mailroom, class of '74. After graduation, Mitch went into production and Elliot went to law school at night while working as a literary agent at the William Morris Agency by day.

When Mitch decided that production was not his forte, he joined Progressive Artists Agency as a theatrical agent until Elliot left WMA, and as Elliot describes it, they "naively and successfully" started the literary department at PAA. In 1981, they opened their own offices and are now recognized as one of the most prestigious, tasteful and successful agencies in town.

KS believes in "30-year-careers" for their clients and they invest the time to nurture beginners whether they are writers or directors. Elliot and Mitch still take time to view and value new talent. Associate Todd Koerner came to KS via United Talent's mailroom and assisting UTA partner Gary Cosay.

KS has been successful in terms of moving talent from one venue to another; Emmy-award winning director, Eric Laneuville was an actor before he started directing. Andy Ackerman was a film editor before he started directing on *Cheers, Wings, Frazier, Ellen*, etc. and is now the resident director for *Seinfeld*. Paul Lazarus went from being a Tony-nominated Broadway director to directing on *LA Law, Melrose Place* and *Dream On* (he got an Ace nomination for that).

Agents
Mitch Kaplan, Elliot Stahler and Todd Koerner.
Client List
12 directors.
Clients
Eric Laneuville, Andy Ackerman, Paul Lazarus and
others.

▓ Joyce Ketay Agency

1501 Broadway #1910
at 46th Street
New York, NY 10036
212-779-2398

Cancer Research Diagnosis and non-profit theater have
produced an unusually synergistic partnership. Joyce
Ketay left the scientific community in search of a less
depressing life. While she decided what to do with herself, a friend suggested work as an assistant to literary
agent Ellen Neuwald. With clients like David Rabe and
John Guare to deal with, Joyce got a taste for quality
right away. When Ellen died in 1980, Joyce started her
own agency (Joyce Ketay Agency) and ran it alone for
10 years. In the fall of 1991, Carl Mulert started working with Joyce.

Originally a production and theater manager
for Arena State and Playwrights Horizons, Carl was
burned out and seeking a new life, when he confided to
old friend Joyce that he wanted a break and a chance to
look for a new direction, maybe he would "find a job
as a secretary in a law firm someplace." Seizing the
opportunity, Joyce talked him into being her assistant
while he was searching. Carl's new direction had found
him: Ketay's business tapped into all the skills he
brought from "the other side of the desk in theater."
Both he and Joyce decided he should take a more
active role. By January of 1993, Carl and Joyce had
became partners.

They represent such important playwrights as
Tony Kushner and Michael Cristofer, as well as
writer/director Stuart Ross (*Forever Plaid*), Ben
Levit, Roberta Levitow, Michael Sexton, Eric

Simonson and others. Joyce and Carl handle writers,
directors and designers.

Agents
Joyce Ketay and Carl Mulert.
Client List
50 writers and directors.
Clients
Stuart Ross, Eric Simonson, Ben Levit,
Roberta Levitow, Michael Sexton and others.

Paul Kohner, Inc.

9300 Wilshire Boulevard #555
just W of Rexford
Beverly Hills, CA 90212
310-550-1060

The late Paul Kohner built this prestigious agency into one of the most successful and famous boutique theatrical agencies in town. His list of actors, writers and directors is filled with famous names from Europe and America. In 1987, a year before Paul died, colleagues Gary Salt and Pearl Wexler bought the agency and continue to deal in the old-world manner with which clients Liv Ullman and Max Van Sydow are familiar.

The literary list of 35 writers and 12 directors contain names like Istvan Szabo (*Meeting Venus, Mephisto*), Donald Westlake (*The Grifters*), John Toles-Bey (*Rage in Harlem*), Tom Clancy (*The Hunt for Red October*), Billy Wilder, etc. Gary heads the literary department repping writers, directors and producers. While finishing a graduate degree at Stanford in the Drama Department in 1972, he got the chance to be trained by ex-MCA-er Ron Leif at Contemporary Korman and entered the agency business.

From there, he moved on to Smith Stevens Associates (now Smith and Associates), where he inaugurated their literary department. After joining Kohner in 1977, his focus has become more and more literary as he carves out a more and more diverse marketplace. He reps publishers, authors, composers, directors, producers, as well as screen and television writers. Colleague BethBohn (The Turtle Agency, Irv Schechter) joins Salt in representing literary clients.

Agents
Gary Salt and Beth Bohn
Client List
65 writers and directors.
Clients
Istvan Szabo, Charles Marowitz, Jim Johnston, Fred
Keller, Donna Pescow, Victor Nunez and others.

■ Don Kopaloff Agency, Inc.

1930 Century Park West #403
in Century City
Los Angeles, CA 90067
310-203-8430

Don Kopaloff started in the business as a messenger for
Twentieth Century Fox in New York. He caught the
eye of Helen Straus, the head of the literary department at William Morris who urged him to attend
William Morris University (the mailroom). Don took
time out for Korea, but was soon back at WMA rub-
bing shoulders with James Michener (before he was
James Michener). He was fortunate to work in almost
every department, which gave him an overview of the
business that would serve him well later as head of
motion pictures for Avco Embassy.

Co-head of motion pictures in New York,
Don's dreams of life in California were fulfilled when
Freddy Fields and David Begelman formed CMA and
invited Don to join them. Later, as head of Avco, he
found new young writers and directors and helped
develop many important films.

Don Burry Management, the agency Don
started in 1971 was so successful that it was bought by
IFA. Don joined his clients there until 1976, when he
opened his own office again.

Agents
Don Kopaloff
Client List
12-14 directors.
Clients
Check DGA listings.

◼ The Lantz Office

888 Seventh Avenue
between 56th & 57th Streets
New York, NY 10106
212-586-0200

The Lantz Office is one of the class acts in the annals
of show biz. When I quizzed New York agents as to
other agents they admired, Robert Lantz was the name
most mentioned. He started in the business as a story
editor. On a Los Angeles business trip from his
London home in 1950, Phil Berg of the famous Berg-
Allenbery Agency made him an offer he couldn't
refuse: "Don't go home. Come to New York. Open a
New York office for us." Mr. Lantz indeed did open
the New York office at 3 East 57th Street and
represented Clark Gable, Madeleine Carroll and other
illustrious stars until William Morris bought that
company a year later.

Lantz worked for smaller agencies for a few
years before opening Robert Lantz, Ltd. in 1954. In
1955, he succumbed to Joe Mankiewicz's pleas and
joined him producing film. It took only three years to
figure out that he found agenting a much more
interesting profession. In 1958, Lantz re-entered the
field as a literary agent. Feeling that a mix of actors and
directors and writers gave each segment more power,
his list soon reflected that.

Dennis Aspland worked for the legendary Sam
Cohn before joining Lantz in representing screen-
writers and directors. The list of directors include
Milos Forman, Adam Davidson, Herb Gardner,
Michael Blakemore, Mike Ockrent and Howard
Davies.

Robert Lantz and Dennis Aspland.
20 directors.
Milos Forman, Adam Davidson, Herb Gardner, Michael Blakemore, Mike Ockrent and Howard Davies.

▆ Major Clients Agency

345 Maple Drive #395
btwn Santa Monica & Burton Way
Beverly Hills, CA 90210
310-205-5000

Founder Leonard Hanzer must have enjoyed his stay
in the army since he named the business he started in
1974 after his rank. Major Talent (as it was known
then) thrived from the beginning and gained access and
prestige when Hanzer became one of the first to
conceive the concept of packaging. As the business
grew, Leonard recruited Paramount television chief,
Richard Weston as his partner. When Hanzer died of a
heart attack six months later, Weston drafted Lorimar
television chief, Jeffrey Benson to help out.

In 1985, two future partners joined the agency.
Diane Fraser left her job at McCartt Oreck & Barrett
to join the MC team and Paramount business affairs
lawyer Stephen Rose decided to change sides of the
desk. Instead of negotiating against writers and directors, he would use those skills and his creativity to
nurture them.

A brief wedding between MC and McCartt,
Oreck and Barrett in 1991 produced a new agency—
Metropolitan Talent Agency. When the wedding
ended in divorce after only two years, Richard,
Jeffrey, Stephen and Diane regrouped and reclaimed
their name.

MC functions as a management team nurturing
clients with concern and hands on relationships.
Stephen feels nourishing alliances produces a synergy
that benefits everyone.

Although this agency's impressive clients are

very far along in the business, Rose tells me he gets great satisfaction from building, managing and developing young careers as well.

Colleagues Steve Marks (ICM) and Ross Fineman (Abrams Artists) join the partners servicing their list of 10-15 directing clients.

Agents
Jeffrey Benson, Richard Weston, Diane Fraser, Stephen Rose, Steve Marks and Ross Fineman.

Client List
10-15 directors.

Clients
Lee Shallat, John Tracy, Fred Gerber, Kim Friedman and others.

Media Artists Group/MAG

8383 Wilshire Boulevard #954
at San Vicente/Nibbler's Building
Los Angeles, CA 90211
213-658-5050

Raphael Berko was a desperate actor when he took a job at The Caroline Leonetti Agency and pretended to be his own agent. Nabbed by SAG for conflict of interest and forced to choose careers, 29-year-old-Raphael became an agent and bought the agency.

Barbara Alexander, who leads the growing literary department has a varied background. She's been a production assistant, a VP of development at Odyssey Films and a writer/director/producer of short films. Colleague Ken Greenblatt was a consultant on Wall Street and a theater general manager.

MAG believes in developing careers and taking clients on for the long haul. The select list of less than half a dozen directors includes Jim Fargo (*Every Which Way but Loose, The Enforcer*) and feature director and producer, Paul Ziller (*Deadly Surveillance, Blood Fist IV*).

Most clients come to this agency through industry referral although Barbara says she has been known to call someone in from a terrific letter. Don't send a reel without permission.

Agents
Barbara Alexander, Ken Greenblatt and Raphael Berko.
Client List
Under 6 directors.
Clients
Paul Ziller, Jim Fargo and others.

▐▀▀ Metropolitan Talent Agency

4526 Wilshire Boulevard
at Rossmore
Los Angeles, CA 90010
213-857-4500

Once a successful actor, owner Chris Barrett says
acting wasn't enough of a challenge, so in mid 1982, he
took a pay cut to train to become an agent. His first
job was as J. Michael Bloom's assistant. By April of
1983, he left Bloom and by that fall, Bettye McCartt,
Mary Oreck and Chris were the proud owners of
McCartt Oreck Barrett, representing some of the most
successful actors in the business.

Briefly partnered with literary force Major
Clients after Mary Oreck left to join Borinstein
Bogart, MOB changed its name to Metropolitan to
reflect the merger. Major Clients withdrew in March
of 1993 and Bettye McCartt moved to The Artists
Agency, leaving Chris as the sole owner.

Still tasteful, elegant and connected, the new
offices on Rossmore reflect the plans Barrett has for his
agency. More important than the physical space, however, is the announcement that superagent Deborah
Miller has come to Metropolitan. Head of Talent at the
William Morris Agency for 15 years, she spent a year
and a half at APA, before moving to Metropolitan.

Andrew Howard joined Metropolitan in 1994
to continue developing the list of directors at this
agency. A lawyer who decided during law school that
he must be involved in show business, Howard worked
for ICM in New York and headed a production
company with Bob Giraldi there. Besides agenting at
WMA, he was a producer with HBO before joining

Metropolitan in late 1994. Colleagues Paul Kelmenson (Camden, ITG), Jeff Okin (David Shapira) and MTA owner Chris Barrett all serve the growing list of directors at this agency.

Agents
Andrew Howard, Paul Kelmenson, Jeff Okin and Chris Barrett.
Client List
5 directors.
Clients
Michele Lee, James Keach and Peter O'Fallon.

◼ WMA/William Morris Agency

1350 Avenue of the Americas
at 48th Street
New York, NY 10019
212-586-5100

Yes, Virginia, there really was a man named William
Morris who started this agency in 1898. The IBM of
the Big Five, WMA has recently gone through major
restructuring in an attempt to compete with #1 (CAA)
and #2 (ICM). In its bid to transform, WMA merged in
late 1992 with Triad in order to capture more big name
actors. Jeff Hunter, Gene Parseghian (the NY partners
of Triad) and Joanna Ross and Frank Frataroli joined
WMA agents Johnny Planco, Emily Gerson, Joan
Fields, Bill Butler and Larry Taube in representing
their combined talent lists.

If your career is heating up and you are so
inclined, venerable William Morris is now in the
position of *really* trying harder, since they are number
three. I'm told by my Los Angeles WMA friends that
the word from on high is to "never take 'no' for an
answer" in pursuing a client's opportunities. The trick
is to become the client WMA is looking to please. My
knowledge of the Triad bunch leads me to believe
chances of person-to-person treatment at WMA have
greatly improved.

The New York office of WMA will be moving
from 1350 Avenue of the Americas to 1325 (about 3
blocks away and fronting on West 53rd), so check to
see if they've moved if you intend to visit their offices.

More on The William Morris Agency

WMA/William Morris Agency

151 El Camino Drive
S of Wilshire
Beverly Hills CA 90212
310-274-7451

in Chapter 9 on Star/Conglomerate Agencies.

Agents
Jeff Hunter, Gene Parseghian, Lee Rosenberg,
John Riley, Scott Zimmerman, Leonard Hirshan,
Arthur Axelman, Alan Izeman, Jeff Field, Rick Hess,
George Lane, Mary Meagher, John Burnham,
Bill Butler, Johnny Planco, Frank Frataroli,
Dave Phillips, Emily Gerson, Joan Fields,
Chris Simonian, John Sheinberg, Greg Lipstone, and
Larry Taube.

Client List
Very large.

Clients
Robert Butler, Arthur Penn, Michael Tolkin,
Peter Barnes, Henry Bromwell, Pamela K. Long,
Anna Sandor, Bruce Vilanch, Noah Stern,
Roger Wilson, Peter Hewitt, Don Scardino,
Diane Wilk, David Wickes, Roger Spottiswoode
and many others.

▦ Helen Merrill

435 W 23rd Street #1A
btwn 8th and 9th Avenues
New York, NY 10011
212-691-5326

One of the most prestigious literary agencies in town
and certainly one of the most difficult to penetrate is
Helen Merrill. Originally a photographer, Merrill
became an agent out of financial necessity, and from
the names on her client list, it's clear that money has
not been a problem since she started her business in
1976. Helen Merrill represents some of the most
important directors, designers, authors, playwrights
and screenwriters in the business and only considers
query letters accompanied by self-addressed, stamped
envelopes. These letters should contain not only brief
descriptions of the project, but productions with the
producers' names attached to it.

Don't inundate this office with material unless
you have the resume to back it up.

Ms. Merrill would not name clients, so my list
is from the SSD&C membership book.

Agents
Helen Merrill and others.
Client List
30 directors.
Clients
Terence Lamude, David Holdgrive, Michael Grief,
Gordon Edelstein, Charles Towers, Charles Newell
and others.

▚ Fifi Oscard Agency

24 W 40th Street 17th floor
W of 5th Avenue
New York, NY 10018
212-764-1100

Fifi Oscard was a frustrated housewife and mother in
1949 when she began working gratis for Lee, Harris,
Draper. When I asked her in what capacity she was
working, she said, "mostly as a jerk" but added that in
nine months she was no longer inept and had worked
herself up to $15 a week. Always interested in theatre
and with the ability "to do almost anything" Fifi
has prospered.

From LHD, Fifi moved to The Lucille Phillips
Agency, working three days a week. That inauspicious
beginning led to Fifi's purchase of LPA in 1959 and the
birth of Fifi Oscard Associates, Inc. This agency deals
with actors, directors, producers, singers, composers,
writers—every arm of showbiz except the variety field.

Fifi still comes into the office every day to
oversee her always successful venture. Bruce Ostler was
at Bret Adams before he came to Fifi, joining Carmen
LaVia in representing the group of about a dozen
always working theater directors. Some from their list
are Stuart Vaughan, Arthur Storch, Mary Zimmerman,
Andrew Traister and the controversial international
director, Robert Woodruff.

Agents
Bruce Ostler and Carmen LaVia.
Client List
12 directors.
Clients
Andrew Traister, Robert Woodruff and others.

The Daniel Ostroff Agency

9200 Sunset Boulevard #402
W of Doheny
Los Angeles, CA 90069
310-278-2020

Daniel Ostroff's advice to young directors and writers is to find a hot new agent and grow up with him. He says that is what happened to him and a look at some of his clients confirms the wisdom of the plan for both writer and agent. Prestigious clients like Michael Blake (*Dances with Wolves*) and Richard Friedenberg (*A River Runs Through It*) are prime examples of clients who were young and scratching at the same time that Daniel was making the journey from the mailroom at ICM to agenting. Daniel moved to Writers & Artists, partnered with Robert Wunsch (Wunsch/Ostroff) and then opened his own office in 1987.

      Other clients include Thom Eberhardt (*Night of the Comet, Honey, I Blew Up the Kids*), Ken Kaufman (*The Air Up There*) and Dave Fuller and Rick Natkin (*Necessary Roughness*) and Josann McGibbon and Sara Parriott (*Runaway Bride*). I swear, he's only got 15 clients and it seems like they are all currently cutting big time deals. Originally from Washington, D. C., Daniel is an excellent illustration of how true the old adage "everyone knows somebody some place and that's how to get into show business" really is. His introduction to the mailroom at ICM came about because his brother lived next door to a television producer.

      In an article in Variety by John Evan Frook (November 5, 1992), Daniel tells a interesting story about success: "Years ago, I read a profile in *The New*

York Times about the world's greatest piano salesman. He worked long hours, played the piano, kept voluminous files...and knew everyone in the music business...I realized the key thing was left out: Yes, he did all of those things but he also sold Steinways. Like him. I sell Steinways."

Don't get excited and compose a query letter. This man is highly committed to the list of clients he already has. He feels agents are being irresponsible to their clients spending time looking for new clients instead of paying attention to the clients they already have. So instead of wasting your time and postage, check out the ideas he offers in Chapter Five.

Agents
Daniel Ostroff
Client List
15 directors.
Clients
Michael Blake, Richard Friedenberg, Thom Eberhardt, Ken Kaufman, Jim McBride, Dave Fuller and Rick Natkin, Josann McGibbon and Sara Parriott and others.

 **paradigm**

a talent and literary agency

10100 Santa Monica Boulevard 25th floor
in Century City
Los Angeles, CA 90067
310-277-4400

In 1969, after 21 collective years interning with various big agencies, Stu Robinson and Bernie Weintraub opened their own offices. Tired of endless staff meetings, wasted time and limited to coverage "west of La Brea," they wanted to represent the whole town and do it "their way." They added partner Ken Gross (Ken Gross Agency) in 1985 and he became a full partner by 1990 (Robinson Weintraub and Gross).

In 1993, RWG became bi-coastal joining the current merger-trend joining two prestigious theatrical agencies, STE and Gores/Fields with the equally impressive literary agency, Shorr, Stille & Associates to form a new mini-conglomerate. Partners at paradigm are Sam Gores, Clifford Stevens, Tex Beha, Stu Robinson, Bernie Weintraub and Ken Gross. A true merger, no agent from any of the three agencies lost a job.

This talented and humanistic list of agents expects to continue intimate family-style representation while reaping the informational rewards of their expanded coverage. Paradigm reps writers, directors, producers, cinematographers, stylists, editors and below-the-line personnel. Clients include writer/director John Sayles (*Brother From Another Planet* and *Eight Men Out*) and Marty Cohan (Co-creator *Who's the Boss?*).

 **paradigm**

a talent and literary agency

200 W 57th Street #900
at 7th Avenue
New York, NY 10019
212-246-1030

Paradigm reps 100-125 writers, directors and producers as well as documentaries, properties of all kinds (series, full length presentations, plays, books, etc.). Paradigm does not accept unsolicited material, so you'll have to find someone who knows someone to gain entree to this important energized addition to the Los Angeles marketplace.

Agents who represent directors at paradigm are Ken Gross, Bernard Weintraub, Gary Pearl, Doug Brodex and Rob Goldenberg.

Agents
Ken Gross, Bernard Weintraub, Gary Pearl, Stu Robinson, Doug Brodex, Kerry Jones and Lucy Stille

Client List
150+ directors and writers.

Clients
Kenneth Branagh, Jeff Harris, Mel Shavelson, James Quinn, John Sayles, Hubert Selby Jr., Maurice David Phillips, Marty Cohan and others.

![clapperboard icon] Paramuse Artists Associates

1414 Avenue of the Americas
at 58th Street
New York, NY 10019
212-758-5055

Shirley Bernstein started in the business as a producer for theater, television and film. Her experiences with agents made her unwilling to even discuss the possibilities of being an agent with the folks from William Morris who kept courting her in the 1960s. Finally, after a television show she had been producing was cancelled, it occurred to her there might be a more stable way of making an income than being a producer. At that point, the distinguished Ted Ashley (IFA) asked Shirley to join his agency. Because Ted Ashley is such a smart, soft-spoken and terrific man, and would allow Shirley to "float" until she decided in which area she wanted to specialize, she succumbed.

As a result, Shirley has a brilliant overview of all parts of the agency business. In 1972 Shirley opened her own office with partner Doris Vidor (the daughter of Harry Warner) with one client, Stephen Schwartz (*Pippin*).

Shirley works alone these days with clients like Joe Stein (*Fiddler on the Roof, Zorba*) and Arthur Laurents (*Gypsy*).

Ms. Bernstein rarely takes on new clients and usually only by referral. Paramuse represents writers, composers, lyricists and directors.

Agents
Shirley Bernstein
Client List
10-15 directors.
Clients
Check DGA and SSDC listings.

◼ Preferred Artists

16633 Ventura Boulevard #1421
2 blocks W of Hayvenhurst
Encino, CA 91436
818-990-0305

Lew Weitzman somehow transmuted himself from a student with a major in Russian at UCLA into a major literary agent. Weitzman's first exposure to the business was via the MCA training program in 1962. Already on the rise, Lew was invited to join distinguished Park Citron (which became Chasin-Park-Citron) when government antitrust laws forced the breakup of MCA. He spent seven years in the motion picture and television literary department of William Morris.

Lew Weitzman and Associates was so prestigious that Taft Broadcasting sought them out and a merger resulted. When American Financial bought that business, Lew was free to start Preferred Artists with partner Roger Strull. The balance of the Preferred team includes Sylvia Hirsch (William Morris) and Susie Weissman (ICM).

Since 1988, Preferred Artists has been representing about 90-100 writers, producers and directors.

Agents
Lew Weitzman, Roger Strull, Sylvia Hirsch and Susie Weissman.
Client List
90-100 writers, producers and directors.
Clients
Robert Vincent O'Neil, Vernon Howard Nobles and others.

■ Jim Preminger Agency

1650 Westwood Boulevard #201
S of Wilshire
Los Angeles CA 90024
310-475-9491

One of the most prestigious literary agencies in town is run by Jim Preminger. Jim's original show-biz goal was to become a producer. He spent three years optioning properties and working with writers on screenplay adaptations, as well as working on a couple of feature film productions, trying to get into the business any way he could. When he approached The Artists Agency with a project he hoped to package for Jack Nicholson (in 1975), they said "no" to the package, but recognizing Preminger's potential, asked him to open their own literary department. Since they made him a partner in 1977, I guess they were pleased.

In 1980, he decided to open his own agency with a dozen clients. At this point, Jim and colleagues Harvey Harrison and Monica Riordan represent about 60 clients covering all principal literary areas: motion pictures, long-form television, series television, plus a number of animation writers as well as clients in interactive media. Of these clients, about 10 are directors, and the balance are writers and/or writer-directors. This is a classy and important agency.

Agents
Jim Preminger, Harvey Harrison and Monica Riordan.
Client List
60 writers and directors.
Clients
Edward G. Rugoff, Stephen M. Hatman and others.

▉ Renaissance/H. N. Swanson, Inc.

8523 Sunset Boulevard
½ block W of La Cienega
Los Angeles, CA 90069
310-652-5385

A strong new literary force joined the Los Angeles
scene when Joel Gotler's prestigious Renaissance
Agency joined celebrated H.N. Swanson in late 1994.

Originally a magazine publisher, H. N.
Swanson (Swanie) was brought to California by David
Selznick as an adviser and a producer. It didn't take
Swanie long to realize there was no West Coast
representation for all the writers that kept getting off
the trains from New York, so he sought to fill the void
when he opened H. N. Swanson, Inc. in 1934. In 1936
he built the building that still houses his progeny,
filled with leather couches, mahogany walls and large
posters of historic clients like Pearl S. Buck, F. Scott
Fitzgerald and Ernest Hemingway.

Swanie is gone now and if HNS had to merge
with anyone, surely Swanie would have loved that his
protege, Joel Gotler is the one. As a matter of fact, Joel
started in the business with Swanie in 1974 and when
Joel decided he wanted to open his own agency four
and a half years later, Swanie lent him the money to do
so.

Swanie's agency foundered for a while after he
died, until stepson, Thomas Shanks, joined the business
in 1989. The agency survived and prospered under his
care and now represents not only famous book authors
and their estates, but a good solid group of film and
television writer and writer-director clients as well.

Agents at R-HNS who represent directors are

Jim Anderson, Irv Schwartz and Larry Kennar. Jim's background includes stints agenting at ICM and development at Paramount. While at ICM, Anderson was influenced by CEO Jeff Berg who firmly believes that directors are the lifeblood of an agency; Jim is seeking to make R-HNS a real contender in that area. Irv Schwartz was at Metropolitan and Larry Kennar came from the Maggie Field Agency.

Directors from the list include Sam Austin, Russ Metzer and Jimmy Zeillenger, Will Curan (*Lie, Cheat and Steal*) and Jamie Bruce (*Dirty Money*).

Agents
Irv Schwartz, Jim Anderson and Larry Kennar.
Client List
6-8 directors.
Clients
Will Curan, Jamie Bruce, Sam Auster, Russ Metzer, Jimmy Zeillenger and others.

▦ Richland/Wunsch/Hohman

9220 Sunset Boulevard #311
W of Doheny
Los Angeles, CA 90069
310-278-1955

Where else can you get an agent who not only pilots his own jet, but is profiled in *Los Angeles Magazine* ferrying around the likes of Burt Reynolds, Henry Winkler and such diverse Presidents as Ronald Reagan and Bill Clinton? Pilot/agent, Dan Richland embodies the spirit of this agency which says, in fact, you can have a real life and still be successful.

Richland ran his own agency before finding like-minded individualist, Bob Wunsch. Wunsch was a VP of production at United Artists, a network executive and an independent film producer (*Slapshot* w/Paul Newman) before he left the agency he had started in 1982 to join up with Richland in 1985.

The third partner, Bob Hohman began his career at The Artists Agency. He became an agent at Stanford Beckett and Associates in 1983 and a partner in 1984. In 1985, Triad beckoned and by 1988, Bob was head of their motion picture literary department.

In 1991, Hohman, Wunsch and Richland went into business together to offer a "small agency environment with big agency entree."

Most of the list of 15 directors started with this agency as writers and have made successful transitions to writer/director status.

Agents
Dan Richland, Bob Wunsch and Bob Hohman.
Client List
15 directors.
Clients
Donald Petrie and others.

▐▐▐ The Marion Rosenberg Office

8428 Melrose Place #C
E of La Cienega Boulevard
Los Angeles CA 90069
213-653-7383

In 1979, Marion was already a successful theater and film producer both here and abroad when super-agent Robby Lantz asked her to open his Los Angeles office. Working for Robby, she got to use all the skills and contacts she had accrued while producing, to promote one of the most luminous client lists in the world.

Ten years later, Marion opened her own prestigious office with a glittering client list. She's adamant about not printing clients' names, so you'll have to check DGA lists. If you don't have a swell resume and an entree, forget about this agency. But it's definitely something to aspire to.

Marion and colleague Matthew Lesher (Henderson Hogan) also represent writers, actors, composers and one costume designer. Matthew basically services the actors while Marion handles the writers and directors.

I've been trying to interview Marion Rosenberg for a long time. When it finally occurred to me to find someone to recommend me, it was no problem at all. This is definitely an office where no one gets a hearing without an entree.

Agents
Marion Rosenberg and Matthew Lesher.
Client List
12 directors.
Clients
Check DGA listings.

▰ Rosenstone/Wender

3 E 48 Street
E of Fifth Avenue
New York, NY 10017
212-832-8330

Howard Rosenstone started in the business with
William Morris in 1963. Originally an actor's agent, he
decided soon enough that he preferred to handle
directors and playwrights. In 1977, he left WMA to
start his own agency (Howard & Company) and in
1980 he teamed with Phyllis Wender to form
Rosenstone/Wender. Wender and Rosenstone each
maintain their own lists and function alone.
　　　　Rosenstone represents directors, orchestrators,
screenwriters, playwrights, composers and lyricists.
Among RW's clients are Jack O'Brien and Graciela
Daniele.

Agents
Howard Rosenstone, Phyllis Wender and Ron
Gwiazola.
Client List
20 directors.
Clients
Jack O'Brien, Graciela Daniele and others.

Schechter (Irv) Company, The

9300 Wilshire Boulevard #201
at Rexford Drive
Beverly Hills, CA 90212
310-278-8070

In 1984, after 15 years at The William Morris Agency, Irv Schechter opened the prestigious agency that today is a full-service company representing writers, directors, actors and below-the-line personnel. Vice-president Debbee Klein left a job assisting Norman Lear and joined Irv shortly after Irv opened his doors, and became an agent at 21.

The literary department at Schechter covers every base: Andrea Simon heads the animation and Saturday morning department, Victorya Michaels handles game shows as well as writers and directors in off-network cable and talk shows, while Irv, Debra Lieb (Triad) and Charlotte Savavi preside over the film department. Debbee, fellow vice-president Don Klein (no relation) and Michael Margules rep the primetime television department. Forward thinking and on top of trends, Debbee speaks to her clients weekly, attends tapings and believes agents should earn their 10%.

Agents
Irv Schechter, Victorya Michaels, Debbee Klein, Don Klein, Charlotte Savavi, Debra Lieb, Andrea Simon and Michael Margules.
Client List
100 writers and directors.
Clients
Arlene Sanford, Starling Price, Thomas O. Richard, David L. Rosenbloom and others.

![clapperboard icon] Shapiro-Lichtman, Inc.

8827 Beverly Boulevard # C
W of La Cienega
Los Angeles, CA 90048
310-859-8877

If you become a client of Shapiro-Lichtman, rest
assured that your phone calls will be returned. Martin
Shapiro was still at the office at 8 o'clock at night
when he returned my call. This is definitely the guy I
would want representing me. Shapiro and Mark
Lichtman were colleagues at General Artists
Corporation in 1968. Martin left when GAC merged
with the forerunner of ICM, CMA. He worked at
both the Phil Gersh and William Morris Agencies
before rejoining with Lichtman to open Shapiro-
Lichtman on Independence Day in 1969. Marty
wouldn't name any clients, lest he leave someone out,
but gave me permission to list some of his prestigious
clients. They include Emmy-winning director Joseph
Sargent *(Miss Rose White)* and David Nutter *(The X
Files)*. When I asked Marty the size of his list, he was
both evasive and articulate, "Not too large to
devote individual and personal attention to our clients
and large enough that we can do all right." In a constantly shifting marketplace, S-L reps clients across the
board from film to reality programming to interactive projects.

Other agents at S-L are Mitchell Stein,
Christine Foster, Marty's father, Bob Shapiro, Michael
Lewis, Peggy Patrick and Lisa Sullivan. Respected
theatrical agent Bud Moss has also joined the lineup,
bringing a prestigious list of actors and expanding
packaging capabilities.

Agents

Martin Shapiro, Mark Lichtman, Mitchell Stein, Christine Foster, Bob Shapiro, Michael Lewis, Peggy Patrick and Lisa Sullivan.

Client List

"Not too large to devote individual and personal attention to our clients and large enough that we can do all right."

Clients

David Webb Peoples, David Richter, Paul Rabwin, Earl Rath, Lee Philips, David Nutter, Joseph Sargent and others.

■ Ken Sherman & Associates

9507 Little Santa Monica
Writers & Artists Building
at Rodeo Drive
Beverly Hills, CA 90210
310-271-8840

If you feel you can read people by their environment (and I'm one of those people who definitely thinks so), you'd have to have Ken Sherman for an agent just on style, because his office is in the coolest building around. The legendary Writers & Artists building in Beverly Hills has Dan Petrie, Ray Bradbury and Digby Diehl (just for starters) as tenants and makes you feel like all the great screenplays from your past must have been written there.

A native Angelino, Ken says he always wanted to be in the business. While working toward his psychology degree from Berkley, Ken spent his summers working for an academy-award winning educational film company as a production manager. Opting for life experience instead of the job the film company offered after graduation, Ken went to Europe, made crepes in a restaurant, did English dubbing for foreign films, worked on various films, and wrote and researched a guide to Paris before returning to LA where he became a reader for Columbia Pictures.

In 1975, he started in the mailroom/agency training program of The William Morris Agency and ultimately represented both actors and directors. After WMA, Sherman worked at The Lantz Office and Paul Kohner, Inc.

In 1989, he opened his own office. His list includes 25-30 feature writers, directors and producers with famous names, as well as those who will be prominent soon. Ken does not accept unsolicited material and is not interested in expanding his client list.

Agents
Ken Sherman
Client List
25-30 writers and directors.
Clients
Check DGA listings.

▄▄ Smith and Associates

121 North San Vicente Boulevard
S of Burton Way
Beverly Hills, CA 90211
213-852-4777

Many other independent agents in town aspire to be
Susan Smith. Distinguished, elegant, and able to keep
superstar clients like Brian Dennehy, Laura Dern and
Kathy Bates happy while still maintaining boutique
status makes Susan Smith a worthy prototype. She
opened her first office in New York in 1970 and has
continued to add distinguished actors to her list.

The literary department, though not as well
known, is every bit as prestigious. In fact, it is so well
thought of, that APA recently lured away previous
literary department head, Justin Dardis.

Not to worry, the literary department is now
in the capable hands of Peter Donaldson, who started
in the business in the mailroom at CAA and has
headed the literary and talent agency, Karen Anthony
& Associates. The literary list includes writers,
novelists and a few directors.

The client list is purposefully select with first-
class clients.

Agents
Peter Donaldson, Joanne Roberts, and Lisa Helsing.
Client List
40 writers and directors.
Clients
Darren Doane and others.

▦ Stone Manners

8091 Selma Avenue
just W of Crescent Heights
just N of Sunset
Los Angeles, CA 90046
213-654-7575

The offspring of a famous British agent, Tim Stone
came to Los Angeles and established his own agency,
UK Management, providing services for British actors
in this country. Although he used his British list as a
base, Tim has expanded way beyond those beginnings.

Scott Manners was a business major with a
talent for golf, who thought he might be a golf pro.
Although the son of a stand-up comic and a June
Taylor dancer, he never considered life as an actor,
much less as an agent. The eldest of five children, he
escaped the lure of show business until cast in a college
play at Irvine where he became interested in acting.

As passionate about acting as he was about golf,
Scott began to study with Jeff Corey, who led him to
truths which not only helped his acting, but also to
agenting as a profession. His lucky clients benefit from
the passion, drive, empathy and intelligence that Corey
helped focus. Scott can sell anything to anyone.

His first agency job was for Fred Amsel, where
he worked as a go-fer. After two months, Fred tossed
him into the deep water of agenting. Not only didn't
Scott sink, he appears to be a strong swimmer.

Manners worked with Rickey Barr at Richard
Dickens Agency before joining Tim Stone and
colleague Larry Masser in 1983. By April 1986, Larry
Masser became a partner (Stone Masser) and by August
of that year, Scott was the third partner (Stone Masser

Manners. Masser left to join APA.)

Stone Manners has been bigger than it is now. A wife and new baby led Scott to re-examine his goals. Now he and Tim have decided that although they want to be powerful agents, they want to find a way to build and represent star caliber clients with a small distinguished office. I'm sure they will. Come to this agency through referral only.

Tim Stone heads the growing literary department and is joined there by colleague Casey Bierer who was in development at Imagine Films and an agent at APA.

Agents
Tim Stone, Scott Manners and Casey Bierer.
Client List
Building
Clients
Check DGA listings.

■ David Shapira & Associates

15301 Ventura Boulevard # 345
W of Sepulveda
Sherman Oaks, CA 91403
818-906-0322

David Shapira's life was changed by an agent's pinstriped suit. En route to life as a lawyer, he encoun-
tered the celebrated agent, Jerry Steiner. David thought
Jerry "looked so elegant in his pinstriped suit" that
David (apparently not aware that even the Yankees
wear pinstripes) decided to be an agent. He quit school
at 17 to work in the mailroom at General Artists
Corporation where he was befriended by Rod Serling
who helped him switch mailrooms (Ashley-Famous)
with a hefty raise to $75 a week.

This was 25 years ago and the rest, as they say,
is history. It took only seven months in the mailroom
before David, figuring "this was going to take too
long," lied about his age (you had to be 21 to make
deals) and became an agent. David has, at various times,
worked with Marty Baum, Meyer Mishkin and Max
Arnow (who cast *Gone with the Wind*). In 1974, David
opened his first office (Goldstein/Shapira). David
maintains a very select client list of actors, directors,
writers and producers. Not for beginners.

Agents
David Shapira, Mike Wise, Peter Giagni, Dan Schrier
and Bobby Littman.
Client List
Check DGA listings.
Clients
Check DGA listings.

▰ Talent East

79 Fifth Avenue
at 16th Street
New York, NY 10003
212-647-1166

Bob Donaghey's first job in the business was as a page with CBS. Before becoming an agent with J. Michael Bloom, Bob was a bookkeeper, a talent coordinator on *The Ed Sullivan Show* and worked at Grey advertising.

He and a friend opened The Lure International Talent Group, Inc., in 1990, but Bob wanted to concentrate on theater, film and television, instead of models, so he to started Talent East in 1992.

Starting his agency with a legit department instead of just commercials, drew casting directors who knew Bob was serious about having quality clients. Today, Talent East also represents clients for entertainment (bands), commercials, print and a budding literary department. Since they are still building, TE works mainly freelance. They don't have many directors, but perhaps that is a plus. Bob is motivated and seems to have connections everywhere.

He has a liaison relationship with The Dott Burns Agency in Tampa.

Agents
Bob Donaghey and Johnny Puma.
Client List
Freelance, so no listing.
Clients
Freelance only.

▶ The Turtle Agency

12456 Ventura Boulevard
at Whitsett
Studio City, CA 91604
818-506-6898

Cindy Turtle's background includes television production in New York and Los Angeles plus breaking ground at the prestigious Eisenbach-Greene-Duchow Agency as their first female agent.

Turtle was Director of Development for Showtime from 1980-1983 before starting the literary department for Los Angeles agent Harry Gold. She left Harry to form a partnership with the late Mike Rosen (Rosen/Turtle Group). In 1990, Cindy started The Turtle Agency.

Turtle represents writers, directors and producers in all areas. Writers make up about two-thirds of their list of 45 clients.

Agents
Cindy Turtle.
Client List
45 writers and directors.
Clients
Check DGA listings.

▟ UTA/United Talent Agency

9560 Wilshire Boulevard #500
at Rodeo Drive
Beverly Hills, CA 90212
213-273-6700

Originally billing themselves as an intimate William
Morris when Leading Artists was founded in 1983 by
James Berkus (IFA), Robert Stein and Gary Cosay
(WMA), the merger with important literary agency
Bauer Benedek created an agency that is hot on the
heels of the big three.

Bauer Benedek was formed by a former
William Morris agent, Marty Bauer, and entertainment
lawyer, Peter Benedek in 1986. Other partners are
Jeremy Zimmer (ICM) and Martin Hurwitz (New
World Entertainment).

Now known as United Talent Agency, this
fearless group has benefited from the demise of
InterTalent and the merger of Triad with William
Morris. United picked up not only talented agents, but
their clients as well.

The main strength here is writers, producers
and directors, but the talent list continues to be
important and growing.

Clients include Frank Darabont, (*Shawshank
Redemption*), Curtis Hanson (*The River Wild*), Jessie
Nelson (*Corrina, Corrina*), Tom Cherones (*Seinfeld*),
Gregory Hoblit (*NYPD Blue*), Beeban Kidron (*Used
People)*, Jonathan Lawton (*Kirina*) and Frank Pierson
(*Citizen Cohn*).

Agents
Robert Stein, James Berkus, Gary Cosay, Marty Bauer,
David Kanter, Robb Rothman, Toby Jaffe,
Risa Gertner, David Schiff, Peter Benedek,
Jeremy Zimmer, Martin Hurwitz, Marty Adelstein,
Judy Hofflund, Pat Dollard, Karen Russel,
Chris Buchanan, Christopher Harbert, Dana Cioffi
and Ilene Feldman.

Client List

Growing

Clients

Jerry W. Rees, Jonathan Lawton, Tom Cherones,
Gregory Hoblit, Richard I. Pearce, Frank Pierson,
Tim Sullivan, George Huang and others.

Wallerstein Kappleman Agency

6399 Wilshire Boulevard #426
at La Jolla, 1 block W of Crescent Heights
Los Angeles, CA 90048
213-782-0225

Lee Kappleman and Michele Wallerstein met in April 1994 and opened their business in May. These women don't kid around! This entrepreneurial duo started with other agendas and along the way found that agenting was their goal. Lee's masters degree in theater from NYU represents her own goal to be a director. An assistant director for two Broadway shows (*Richard III* and *The Basic Training of Pavlo Hummel* with Al Pacino) and brief internships at the Arena Stage in Washington, D. C. convinced her that the opportunities for women in directing (worse then than now) were too limited for a regular paycheck. So she became an assistant to Bernie Safronski and Freddi Rappaport, the heads of drama and variety specials at CBS Entertainment.

Within a year, she was put in their year long executive training program, "probably the most thorough education in network programming available." She spent six weeks in every division, learning how the network does its programming, shapes its advertising and researches and tests its shows. CBS then moved Lee to Los Angeles where she spent a couple of years working with some of the best people in the business doing movies of the week. From CBS, she moved into a job developing programs for name television actresses that introduced her to literary agents and her new profession.

"Writing is the absolute hub of all creativity in

---

this business because the word begins everything." Since her life as a buyer had divorced Lee from her own earlier creative urges, she decided it was time to nourish them by taking her knowledge and contacts to a creative climate. Querying agencies who would take her without a list, she found a happy and successful home with McCartt Oreck and Barrett, where she created the literary department in 1985. She moved to APA in 1989 where she was a literary agent in the feature department.

When APA head Marty Klein died, Lee worked briefly with Joel Gotler at The Renaissance Agency. When she decided she didn't want to be limited to assigned territories, she opened her own business in order to have access to the whole town.

Michele Wallerstein also took a long time to figure out what she wanted to be when she grew up. She worked in the music business for a while helping start Pulsar Records (a subsidiary of Mercury records). She then worked with ABC Dunhill before falling into a job as a secretary at the literary department of ICM (in 1975, when it was still IFA). From that moment on, she knew she had found her career. She wanted to be an agent. Her first client, Michael McGreevey, is still with her today.

It took Michele six years to become an agent. Along her journey through five or six agencies, she realized she wasn't happy with agents and the way they operated and decided to open her own business. She opened The Wallerstein Company in 1980, representing writers, producers, directors, actors and authors. The writers strike in 1988 took its toll and she finally threw in the towel and joined Preferred Artists. She was working at H. N. Swanson, when she met Lee.

Wallerstein Kappleman represent directors, writers, producers, novelists and special effects producers. They also handle rights to true life stories, i.e. Tonya Harding and the like.

Although more of their clients are writers and writer-producers than directors, they do represent directors and are looking to add to that list. Check Michele's quotes elsewhere to see what you should have before querying.

Agents
Michele Wallerstein and Lee Kappleman.
Client List
50 writers and directors.
Clients
Brian Trenchard-Smith, Charles Dennis, Richard Danus and others.

▓▓ Wile Enterprises, Inc.

2730 Wilshire Boulevard #500
at Harvard Street
Santa Monica, CA 90403
310-826-9768

Shelley Wile is one of the few graduates of William
Morris University who did not start in the mailroom.
A "failed actor," Shelly says a friend led him by the
hand to WMA where he started as a secretary in the
literary department in television live dramatic action.
Shelly's background in theater propelled his career
from secretary to agent within a year. Then, CMA
(forerunner of ICM) hired him away to run their
literary department. He withdrew from the agency
business to become a vice-president of development of
feature films for television for Cinema Center Films.
In 1971, Shelley left to develop shows for Talent
Associates with David Suskind and Leonard Stern. By
1974 he was lured back to the agency business by
Adams Ray Rosenberg. Thought by many to be the
most prestigious boutique literary office in Los
Angeles, ARR merged with Triad in 1984 and Shelley
went with them. Triad has now merged with William
Morris and Shelley started his own company in 1989.

   Although Shelley was adamant about not
mentioning the size of his client list or any names, a
quick check at the DGA will reveal a list of heavy
hitters. Sharon A. (Sam) Markevich, (CAA, WMA) is
Shelley's colleague.

   If you are interested in representation from this
office, important industry referrals (by someone who
has *seen* your work) is the only entree.

   This office represents writers, producers and

---

directors although the major thrust is definitely writers.

Agents
Shelley Wile and Sharon A. Markevich.
Client List
Confidential
Clients
Check DGA listings.

▓▒ Writers & Artists

924 Westwood Boulevard #900
at Le Conte by UCLA
Los Angeles, CA 90024
310-824-6300

Joan Scott created this agency (Joan Scott Agency) in 1971 to represent actors. When she expanded the concept to include a literary department, she adopted the present name to reflect the change. She may need to add Etc. to the title because, in 1994, this forward-thinking, prestigious agency added two new departments: the below-the-line division represents production designers, editors and cinematographers and the creative affairs division tracks projects as well as acquires material for representation. All things considered, there doesn't seem to be anything W&A doesn't do.

The new additions reflect the more corporate stance independent agencies have adopted to compete with the big three in a changing industry.

In late 1994 another critical change occurred when the prestigious head of the literary department, Rima Greer, left to open her own agency, Above the Line. She took a lot of writers and directors with her, so it's possible that successor, Lisa Feinstein, will be looking to add to W&A's client list. There are 88 writers and directors on the combined NY/LA lists. About 75% are writers and the directors write as well. Directors in the New York office are represented by department head Bill Craver and colleague Scott Hudson.

◼ Writers & Artists

19 W 44th Street
just W of Fifth Avenue
New York NY 10036
212-391-1112

A heavy hitter in all departments, W&A combines prestige with hands on service. Writers & Artists doesn't look at unsolicited reels.

Agents
Lisa Feinstein, Bill Carver and Scott Hudson.
Client List
88 (NY/LA) writers and directors.
Clients
Monte Merrick, Greg Taylor, Jim Strain, D. A. Dorwart, Philip Cusack, James Melton and others.

■ Stella Zadeh & Associates

11759 Iowa Avenue
at Barrington
Los Angeles, CA 90025
310-207-4114

When Stella Zadeh was an executive for CBS years ago, several colleagues told her she had too much energy for CBS and suggested she start her own business. A year later (in 1985) she was encouraged to start her own talent agency and Richard Lawrence gave her a start. In 1986, she acquired a talent and literary license and the world will never be the same. Somehow (with the help of two assistants), she manages to represent a base list of 80 clients and helps many more. The queen agent of reality-based producers-writers-directors, Stella didn't want me to name names, but says she "has someone" on almost every major talk or magazine show on television.

Don't rush to the mailbox. She only accepts industry referrals, but she will accept query letters. Although she handles a few traditional scriptwriters and directors, the majority of her clients are those whose major thrust is reality-based programming. If you ask me, CBS should have harnessed the energy themselves.

Agents
Stella Zadeh
Client List
85 writers and directors.
Clients
Confidential

12 Glossary

Above-the-line — a budgetary term referring to talent, advertising and other negotiable expenses involved in making a film. This includes writers, directors, actors and producers.

Academy Players Directory — Directory of actors listing pictures and representation.

AD — Assistant Director.

Associate producer — Performs one or more producer functions as delegated by the producer.

Below-the-line — budgetary term referring to production costs including such personnel as gaffers, grips, set designers, make-up, etc. Generally those fees that are not negotiated.

Buzz — Industry term meaning exciting information that everybody is talking about.

Calling card — A spec reel that gets you in the door, shows your most salable strength. Is hopefully short.

Clout — Power.

Connected — An individual who is in the system and has entree to helpful relationships. If I am Mike Ovitz's secretary, I am *connected* to him and could get a project to him, etc.

Co-producers — Two or more producers who perform the producer functions as a team.

Coverage — Report supplied by reader to the buyer.

Development — Process involving writers presenting work and/or ideas to producers and/or directors who oversee the *developing* script through various stages.

The Directors Guild of America — Directors' union — negotiates collective bargaining for directors, arbitrates, provides services of all kinds.

DGA Directory — listing of DGA members, contacts (agents/managers/lawyers) and credits.

Element — According to *The New York Times*, "an element is the basic building block of Hollywood, without which any project is simply an empty space pierced only by the phone calls of agents. Elements may be actors, directors, occasionally producers."

Executive producer — supervises one or more producers.

Half-hour — Situation comedy.

Industrials — Short films produced by special interest groups to sell a product whether it is business, education or the government.

Interactive television — Programming involving audience participation via computer/television sets. Still in its infancy. Said to be the next big thing.

Long-form television — Movies for television.

Line producer — Supervises physical production of project and is supervised by another producer who handles other duties.

Observing — A new director trying to break into television observes another director during the process of producing a project, frequently a half-hour situation comedy. Consists of attending all rehearsals and tapings, sometimes sitting in on casting, story conferences and note sessions. In New York, this is called *trailing.*

Plugged in — Industry slang implying close associations or relationships with those in power.

Producer — Person who initiates, coordinates, supervises and controls all aspects of the process from inception to completion.

PA — Production assistant. A production assistant does whatever needs doing on a production.

Pitch — Term used to define the process where a writer meets with producer(s) to tell the story (pitch) of his idea in hopes he will be hired to write a script.

Query letter — A letter that introduces the director, synopsizes his career and reel and invites further contact, hopefully in four paragraphs or less.

Reader — A person employed by a buyer to weed through many scripts to select which material warrants closer scrutiny.

Rider D— Paragraph 3 states: *90-Day Clause: If during any period of ninety (90) consecutive days immediately preceding the giving of notice of termination herein described, the Director fails to be employed or fails to receive a bona fide offer, then either Director or Agent may terminate the employment of Agent hereunder by giving notice of termination to either party subject to certain terms and provisions.* There are several provisions listed under this. You should obtain a copy of the form from the Guild.

S.A.S.E. — Self addressed stamped envelope — needs to accompany query letters and manuscripts.

Spec scripts — A script written on speculation without any financial remuneration up front or any prior interest from a prospective buyer.

Story analyst — see Reader.

Trailing — see Observing.

Think — Slang term meaning a way of thinking.

The trades — *Daily Variety, The Hollywood Reporter,* and *Weekly Variety* are all newspapers that deal with the entertainment business. Available at newsstands or by subscription.

Treatment — detailed written breakdown of a script — usually scene by scene.

The Writers Guild of America — Screenwriters' union — negotiates collective bargaining for screenwriters, arbitrates, provides services of all kinds.

WGA Directory — listing of WGA members, contacts (agents/managers/lawyers) and credits.

1st — first assistant director.

2nd — second assistant director.

Index to Agents and Agencies

Above the Line Agency, 10, 14, 29, 33, 114, 147, 150, 167, 254

Abrams Harris & Goldberg, 200

Abrams, Robert, 200

Adams Ray Rosenberg, 252

Adams, Bret, 168, 187, 221

Adelstein, Marty, 248

Agency for the Performing Arts, 170

Agency, The, 169, 173, 177

Alessi, Anna Maria, 171

Alexander, Barbara, 149, 215

Amsel, Fred, 242

Anderson, Jim, 230, 231

Angle, Tim, 181

APA, 170, 176, 177, 180, 250

Arlook, Richard, 196

Artists Agency, 172, 216, 229, 232

Artists Group, 173

Ashley, Ted, 226

Ashley-Famous, 183, 202, 244

Aspland, Dennis, 211

Barr, Rickey, 242

Barrett, Chris, 217

Barry Douglas Agency, 187

Bauer, Marty, 247

Baum, Martin, 141, 244

BDP & Associates, 175

Beakel, Walter, 175

Becsey Wisdom Kalajian, 177

Becsey, Laurence S., 169, 177

Becsey·Wisdom·Kalajian, 169, 177

Benedek, Peter, 247

Benson, Jeffrey, 214

Berg, Jeff, 202
Berg, Phil, 211
Berg-Allenbery Agency, 211
Berko, Raphael, 115, 215
Berkus, James, 247
Berman, Richard, 169, 177
Bernstein, Shirley, 226
Bickel, Glenn, 186
Bierer, Casey, 243
Black, Michael, 203
Block, Bill, 142, 202
Bloom, J. Michael, 216
Bohn, Beth, 209
Bohrman, Karen, 195
Borinstein Bogart, 216
Brandt Co., 176
Brandt, Geoffrey, 176
Bresler, Sandy, 172
Bresler, Wolff, Cota, and Livingston, 172
Broder Kurland, 178
Broder, Bob, 178
Broder·Kurland·Webb·Uffner, 120, 121, 127, 151, 178
Brodex, Doug, 225
Buchanan, Chris, 248
Buchwald & Associates, 180, 181
Buchwald & Associates, Don, 197
Buchwald, Don, 180, 181
CAA, 133, 137, 138, 140, 202, 252
CAA/Creative Artists Agency , 185
Carver, Bill, 255
Chasin, Tom, 177
Chasin-Park-Citron, 228
Chech, Judy, 194
Ching, Traci, 181
Cioffi, Dana, 248

CMA, 179, 182, 237, 252

Cohn, Sam, 202, 211

Connolly, Justin, 186

Contemporary Artists, 182

Contempory Korman, 182

Cooper Agency , 183

Cooper, Frank, 183

Cooper, Jeff, 184

Corday, Evan, 198, 199

Cosay, Gary, 247

Cota, Jimmy, 172

Craver, Bill, 254

Curren, Ellen, 197

Dardis, Justin, 241

David Shapira & Associates, 244

Davis, Diane, 198

Despoto, Bill, 189

DGRW, 22, 24, 25, 69

Dinstman, Lee, 171

Directors Company, 5, 33

Directors Network, 188

Dollard, Pat, 248

Don Buchwald & Associates, 180

Don Kopaloff Agency, Inc., 210

Donaghey, Bob, 245

Donaldson, Peter, 241

Douglas Agency, Barry, 187

Douglas, Barry, 22, 24, 25, 61, 69, 187

Douglas, Bill, 203

Douroux & Co., 190

Douroux, Michael, 29, 50, 57, 61, 103, 104, 113, 122,
135, 150, 190

Duva, Robert, 191

Duva-Flack, 191

Eisenbach-Greene-Duchow, 246

Epstein, Gary, 193

Epstein/Wyckoff & Associates, 192, 193

Fair Warning/ICM , 202
Feinstein, Lisa, 254, 255
Feldman, Ilene, 248
Field, Maggie, 119, 194
Fifi Oscard Agency, 221
Fineman, Ross, 214
Flack, Elin, 191
Foster, Christine, 237
Fraser, Diane, 214
Freiberg, Mickey, 172
GAC, 244
Gage Group, 195
Gage, Martin, 195
Gaines, John, 170
Gelff, Laya, 4
General Artists Corporation, 237, 244
Gersh Agency, 196
Gersh Agency New York, 197
Gersh, David, 196
Gersh, Phil, 196, 237
Gertner, Risa, 248
Gladstone, Emile, 169
Gold and Associates, Harry, 173
Gold Marshak and Associates, 198
Gold, Harry, 198, 246
Goldberg, Howard, 200
Goldberg, Susie, 189
Goldenberg, Rob, 225
Goldsmith, Elaine, 141
Goldstein/Shapira, 244
Gomez, Rhonda, 179
Gomez-Quinones, Rhonda, 179
Gores, Sam, 224
Gores/Fields, 224
Gorman, Fred, 187
Gotler, Joel, 250
Grant, Susan, 173, 174

Greenblatt, David, 143
Greenfield, Debra, 141
Greenspan, Alan, 203
Greenstein, Ian, 179
Greer, Rima, 10, 14, 114, 147, 150, 167, 254
Gross, Ken, 224
Guc, David, 197
Gwiazola, Ron, 235
H. N. Swanson, Inc., 230
Haber, Bill, 185
Hanzer, Leonard, 178, 213
Harbert, Christopher, 248
Hardin, Mary, 168
Harris, J. J. , 143
Harris, Scott, 200
Harrison, Harvey, 229
Harry Gold Agency, 198
Hart, Bill, 182
Helen Merrill, 220
Helsing, Lisa, 241
Henderson Hogan, 234
Hirsch, Sylvia, 228
Hofflund, Judy, 143, 248
Hohman, Bob, 103, 105, 114, 121, 125, 126, 135-137,
    146, 148, 151, 232
Holston, Rand, 186
Howard & Company, 235
Howard, Andrew, 217
Howard, Toni, 141, 203
Hudson, Scott, 254, 255
Hunter, Jeff, 138
Hurwitz, Martin, 247
ICM, 138, 140, 141, 177, 183, 187, 202, 222, 228, 237,
    247, 250, 252
ICM International, 202
ICM/International Creative Management , 202
IFA, 178, 179, 226, 247, 250

Innovative Artists , 200
InterTalent, 142, 202, 247
Irv Schechter Company, 7
J. Michael Bloom, 216
Jaffe, Toby, 248
Jennett, Renee, 180
Joan Scott Agency, 254
Jones, Kerry, 225
Joyce Ketay, 207
Kalajian, Jerry, 177
Kalodner, David, 170
Kane, Merrily, 172
Kanter, David, 248
Kaplan Stahler, 6, 101, 204
Kaplan, Mitch, 205
Kappleman, Lee, 249
Karen Anthony & Associates, 241
Kaufman, Bruce, 179
Keele, Lee, 196
Kelly, Maryann, 196
Kelmenson, Paul, 217
Kennar, Larry, 231
Ketay, Joyce, 206
Klein, Debbee, 7, 236
Klein, Don, 236
Klein, Marty, 170, 250
Koerner, Todd, 205
Kohner, Inc., 3, 68, 119, 120, 208
Kopaloff, Don, 210
Korman, Tom, 170
Krentzman, Adam, 186
Kumen-Olenick, 173
Kurland, Norman, 178
Lake & Douroux, 190
Lantz Office, 211, 239
Lantz, Robby, 211, 234
Larner, Lionel, 187

Laurence S. Becsey Agency, 177
Lawrence, Richard, 256
Lee, Harris, Draper, 221
Lefkowitz, Jim, 196
Leif, Ron, 182
Lesher, Matthew, 234
Lewis, Michael, 237
Lewis, Steve, 5, 33, 189
Lichtman, Marty, 237
Lieb, Debra, 236
Limato, Ed, 202
Lionel Larner, 187
Livingston, Mike, 172
Lonner, David, 186
Lourd, Brian, 186
Lucille Phillips Agency, 221
Lure International Talent Group, Inc. , 245
MAG, 215
Maggie Field Agency, 194
Major Clients Agency, 34, 104, 128, 213, 216
Major Talent, 178, 213
Malcolm, Robert, 173
Manners, Scott, 242
Margules, Michael, 236
Marion Rosenberg Office, 234
Marks, Steve, 214
Marshak, Daryl, 198, 199
Marshak/Wyckoff, 198
MCA, 210, 228
McCartt Oreck Barrett, 213, 216, 250
McCartt, Bettye, 216
McNeil, Tim, 180
Meagher, Mary, 197
Mechanic, Nick, 169
Media Artists Group, 115, 149, 215
Melnick, Jeff, 198, 199
Menchel, Michael, 186

Metropolitan Talent Agency, 213, 216
Michaels, Victorya, 236
Miller, Deborah, 216
Milner, Joel, 179
Mishkin, Meyer, 244
Moore, Wanda, 195
Morgan, Walter, 169
Morris, William, 183
Mulert, Carl, 206
Nethercott, Gayla, 179
Neuwald, Ellen, 206
Nigrosh, Nancy, 196
O'Connor, David, 186
Okin, Jeff, 217
Oreck, Mary, 216
Oscard, Fifi, 221
Ostroff Agency, Daniel, 222
Ostroff, Daniel, 222
Ovitz, Mike, 133, 140, 163, 185
paradigm, 47, 100, 101, 121, 122, 190, 224, 225
Paramuse Artists Associates, 226
Park-Citron, 228
Parseghian, Gene, 139
Patman, Andy, 172
Patrick, Peggy, 237
Paul Kohner, Inc., 3, 68, 109, 119, 120, 147, 151, 208,
        239
Paull, Morgan, 175
Pearl, Gary, 225
Perkins, Rowland, 185
Phil Gersh, 237
Pleshette & Green, 146
Pleshette, Lynn, 146
Preferred Artists, 228
Preminger Agency, 229
Preminger, Jim, 11, 23, 59, 107, 109, 113, 136, 229
Progressive Artists Agency, 204

Puma, Johnny, 245
Rapke, Jack , 186
Renaissance Agency, 250
Richard Dickens Agency, 242
Richland, Dan, 232
Richland/Wunsch/Hohman, 103, 114, 121, 125, 126,
    135, 137, 146, 148, 151, 195, 232
Rima Greer, 29, 33
Riordan, Monica, 229
Robert Light Agency, 198
Roberts, Joanne, 241
Robinson Weintraub, 190, 194
Robinson Weintraub and Gross, 224
Robinson, Stu, 32, 35, 47, 68, 100, 101, 110, 120-122,
    190, 224
Rose, Stephen, 24, 34, 50, 54, 104, 128, 214
Rosen, Mike, 246
Rosen/Turtle Group, 246
Rosenberg, Marion, 234
Rosenfield, Michael, 185
Rosenfield, Sonya, 186
Rosenstone, Howard, 235
Rosenstone/Wender, 235
Ross, Eric, 187
Rothacker & Wilhelm, Inc., 187
Rothacker, Flo, 187
Rothacker, Katy, 170
Russel, Karen, 248
Rutter, Art, 173
Salt, Gary, 3, 68, 109, 119, 120, 133, 147, 151, 209
Sandy Bresler Agency, 172
Saunders, David, 171
Savavi, Charlotte, 236
Schechter (Irv) Company, The, 236
Schiff, David, 143, 248
Scott, Joan, 254
Shanks, Thomas, 230

Shapira & Associates, 244
Shapira, David, 244
Shapiro Lichtman, 237
Shapiro, Bob, 237
Shapiro, Marty, 30, 32, 33, 36, 99, 100, 113, 128, 149,
        151, 237
Shapiro, Risa, 141
Shapiro-Lichtman, 30, 32, 33, 36, 128, 149
Shepherd, Dick, 172
Sherman & Associates, 239
Sherman, Ken, 99, 104, 111, 114, 239
Shorr, Stille & Associates, 224
Simon, Andrea, 236
Sindell, Jane, 186
Smith and Associates, 208, 241
Smith Stevens Associates, 208
Smith, Susan, 241
Smith, Todd, 186
Soloway, Arnold, 173
Stahler, Elliot, 5, 6, 101, 103, 123, 143, 205
Stalmaster, Hal, 173, 174
Stanford Beckett and Associates, 232
STE, 224
Stein, Mitchell, 237
Stein, Robert, 247
Steiner, Jerry, 244
Stella Zadeh & Associates, 256
Stevens, Clifford, 224
Stille, Lucy, 225
Stone Manners, 242
Stone Masser , 242
Stone Masser Manners, 242
Stone, Tim, 242
Strain Jennett, 180
Straus, Helen, 210
Strull, Roger, 228
Sullivan, Lisa, 237

Susan Smith Associates, 173
Swedlin, Rosalie, 186
Talent East, 245
Talent Management International, 177
Tellez, Steve, 170
Tenzer, David, 186
The Kohner Agency, 133
Triad, 142, 169, 247, 252
Turtle Agency, 246
Turtle, Cindy, 246
Twentieth Century Artists, 198
Uffner, Beth, 179
United Talent Agency, 247
UTA, 138, 142, 204
UTA/United Talent Agency, 247
Van Dyke, Walter, 169
Wakefield, Karen, 193
Wallerstein Kappleman, 24, 29, 36, 102, 150, 155, 249
Wallerstein, Michele, 24, 29, 36, 102, 150, 155, 249, 251
Ward, James, 201
Wasted Talent, 202
Webb, Elliot, 111, 120, 121, 127, 151
Weinberg, Sandy, 201
Weintraub, Bernie, 224
Weissman, Susie, 228
Weitzman, Lew, 228
Wender, Phyllis, 235
Weston, Richard, 214
Westover, Jonathan, 102, 125, 195
Wexler, Pearl, 208
Wiatt, Jim, 203
Wile Enterprises, Inc., 252
Wile, Shelley, 253
Wilhelm, Jim, 187
William Morris Agency, 218
William Schuller Agency, 169, 177
Wisdom, Victoria, 177

WMA, 133, 137, 140, 167, 173, 176-178, 185, 202, 204, 210, 216, 218, 228, 235-237, 252
Wolff, Don, 172
Wright, Ann, 187
Writers & Artists, 167, 194, 254
Wuliger, Frank, 201
Wunsch, Bob, 232
Wunsch/Ostroff, 222
Wyckoff, Craig, 192
Yoselow, Scott, 197
Zadeh, Stella , 256
Zeigler Ross, 194
Zeitman, Jerome, 169, 177
Zimmer, Jeremy, 247

▣ Index to Los Angeles Agents & Agencies

Above the Line Agency, 10, 167
Adelstein, Marty, 248
Agency for the Performing Arts, 170
Agency, The, 169
Alexander, Barbara, 149, 215
Anderson, Jim, 230, 231
APA, 170, 243
Arlook, Richard, 196
Artists Agency, 172
Artists Group, 173
Barrett, Chris, 217
Bauer Benedek, 247
Bauer, Marty, 247
BDP & Associates, 175
Becsey, Laurence S., 177
Becsey·Wisdom·Kalajian, 177
Beha, Tex, 224
Benedek, Peter, 247
Benson, Jeffrey, 214
Berg, Jeff, 202
Berko, Raphael, 115, 215
Berkus, James, 247
Bickel, Glenn, 186
Bierer, Casey, 243
Block, Bill, 202
Bohn, Beth, 209
Brandt Co., 176
Brandt, Geoffrey, 176
Broder, Bob, 178
Broder·Kurland·Webb·Uffner, 111, 127, 151

Brodex, Doug, 225
Buchanan, Chris, 248
Buchwald & Associates, 180
CAA/Creative Artists Agency , 185
Chech, Judy, 194
Cioffi, Dana, 248
Connolly, Justin, 186
Contemporary Artists, 182
Cooper Agency , 183
Cooper, Frank, 183
Cooper, Jeff, 184
Corday, Evan, 198, 199
Cosay, Gary, 247
Cota, Jimmy, 172
Craver, Bill, 254
Curtis Brown, 198
David Shapira & Associates, 244
Despoto, Bill, 189
Dinstman, Lee, 171
Directors Company, 5, 33
Directors Network, 188
Dollard, Pat, 248
Donaldson, Peter, 241
Douglas, Bill, 203
Douroux & Co., 190
Douroux, Michael, 29, 50, 57, 61, 103, 104, 113, 122,
        135, 150, 191
Epstein/Wyckoff & Associates, 192, 193
Feinstein, Lisa, 254, 255
Feldman, Ilene, 248
Field, Maggie, 119, 194
Fineman, Ross, 214
Foster, Christine, 237
Fraser, Diane, 214
Freiberg, Mickey, 172
Gage Group, 195
Gage, Martin, 195

General Artists Corporation, 244
Gersh Agency, 196
Gersh, David, 196
Gersh, Phil, 196
Gertner, Risa, 248
Gladstone, Emile, 169
Gold Marshak and Associates, 198
Goldberg, Howard, 200
Goldberg, Susie, 189
Gomez, Rhonda, 179
Gomez-Quinones, Rhonda, 179
Gores, Sam, 224
Grant, Susan, 173, 174
Greenblatt, Ken, 215
Greenstein, Ian, 179
Greer, Rima, 14, 114, 147, 167
Gross, Ken, 224
H. N. Swanson, Inc., 230
Haber, Bill, 185
Hanzer, Leonard, 213
Harbert, Christopher, 248
Harris, Scott, 200
Harrison, Harvey, 229
Hart, Bill, 182
Helsing, Lisa, 241
Hirsch, Sylvia, 228
Hofflund, Judy, 248
Hohman, Bob, 103, 105, 114, 121, 125, 126, 135-137,
        146, 148, 151, 232
Holston, Rand, 186
Howard, Andrew, 217
Howard, Toni, 203
Hurwitz, Martin, 247
ICM, 202
ICM/International Creative Management , 202
Innovative Artists , 200
Irv Schechter Company, 7

Jaffe, Toby, 248
Jennett, Renee, 180
Jones, Kerry, 225
Kalajian, Jerry, 177, 178
Kane, Merrily, 172
Kanter, David, 248
Kaplan Stahler, 101, 204
Kaplan, Mitch, 205
Kappleman, Lee, 249
Kaufman, Bruce, 179
Keele, Lee, 196
Kelly, Maryann, 196
Kelmenson, Paul, 217
Kennar, Larry, 231
Klein, Debbee, 7, 236
Klein, Don, 236
Koerner, Todd, 205
Kohner, Inc., 3, 68, 109, 208
Kopaloff, Don, 210
Krentzman, Adam, 186
Kurland, Norman, 178
Lawrence, Richard, 256
Lefkowitz, Jim, 196
Leif, Ron, 182
Lesher, Matthew, 234
Lewis, Michael, 237
Lewis, Steve, 33, 189
Lichtman, Marty, 237
Lieb, Debra, 236
Limato, Ed, 202
Livingston, Mike, 172
Lonner, David, 186
Lourd, Brian, 186
Maggie Field Agency, 194
Major Clients Agency, 34, 128, 213
Malcolm, Robert, 173
Manners, Scott, 242

Margules, Michael, 236
Marion Rosenberg Office, 234
Marks, Steve, 214
Marshak, Daryl, 198, 199
McNeil, Tim, 180
Mechanic, Nick, 169
Media Artists Group, 115, 149, 215
Melnick, Jeff, 198, 199
Menchel, Michael, 186
Metropolitan Talent Agency, 216
Michaels, Victorya, 236
Milner, Joel, 179
Moore, Wanda, 195
Morgan, Walter, 169
Morris, William, 183
Nethercott, Gayla, 179
Nigrosh, Nancy, 196
O'Connor, David, 186
Okin, Jeff, 217
Ostroff Agency, Daniel, 222
Ostroff, Daniel, 222
Ovitz, Mike, 185
paradigm, 47, 100, 101, 121, 122, 224, 225
Patman, Andy, 172
Patrick, Peggy, 237
Paul Kohner, Inc., 3, 68, 109, 119, 120, 147, 151, 208
Pearl, Gary, 225
Perkins, Rowland, 185
Pleshette & Green, 146
Pleshette, Lynn, 146
Preferred Artists, 228
Preminger Agency, 229
Preminger, Jim, 11, 23, 59, 107, 109, 113, 136, 229
Puma, Johnny, 245
Rapke, Jack , 186
Richland, Dan, 232
Richland/Wunsch/Hohman, 103, 105, 114, 121, 125,

126, 135, 136, 146, 148, 151, 232
Rima Greer, 29, 33
Riordan, Monica, 229
Roberts, Joanne, 241
Robinson Weintraub, 190
Robinson Weintraub and Gross, 224
Robinson, Stu, 32, 35, 47, 68, 100, 101, 120-122, 190, 224
Rose, Stephen, 34, 128, 214
Rosenberg Office, Marion, 234
Rosenberg, Marion, 234
Rosenfield, Michael, 185
Rosenfield, Sonya, 186
Rothacker, Katy, 170
Russel, Karen, 248
Rutter, Art, 173
Salt, Gary, 3, 68, 109, 119, 120, 133, 147, 151, 209
Savavi, Charlotte, 236
Schechter (Irv) Company, The, 236
Schiff, David, 248
Scott, Joan, 254
Shanks, Thomas, 230
Shapira & Associates, 244
Shapira, David, 244
Shapiro Lichtman, 237
Shapiro, Bob, 237
Shapiro, Marty, 30, 32, 33, 36, 99, 100, 113, 128, 149, 237
Shapiro-Lichtman, 30, 32, 33, 128
Shepherd, Dick, 172
Sherman & Associates, Ken, 239
Sherman, Ken, 99, 104, 111, 114, 239
Simon, Andrea, 236
Sindell, Jane, 186
Smith and Associates, 241
Smith Stevens Associates, 208
Smith, Todd, 186

Stahler, Elliot, 6, 101, 123, 205
Stalmaster, Hal, 173, 174
Stein, Mitchell, 237
Stein, Robert, 247
Stevens, Clifford, 224
Stille, Lucy, 225
Stockfish, Tammy, 179
Stone Manners, 242
Stone, Tim, 242
Sullivan, Lisa, 237
Swedlin, Rosalie, 186
Tenzer, David, 186
The Kohner Agency, 133
Turtle Agency, 246
Turtle, Cindy, 246
Uffner, Beth, 179
United Talent Agency, 247
UTA/United Talent Agency, 247
Van Dyke, Walter, 169
Wakefield, Karen, 193
Wallerstein Kappleman, 24, 29, 36, 102, 150, 155, 249
Wallerstein, Michele, 24, 29, 36, 102, 155
Ward, James, 201
Webb, Elliot, 111, 120, 121, 127, 151, 178
Weinberg, Sandy, 201
Weintraub, Bernie, 190, 224
Weissman, Susie, 228
Weitzman, Lew, 228
Weston, Richard, 214
Westover, Jonathan, 102, 125, 195
Wexler, Pearl, 208
Wiatt, Jim, 203
Wile Enterprises, Inc., 252
Wile, Shelley, 253
William Morris Agency, 218
Wisdom, Victoria, 177
WMA, 140, 183, 218, 247

Wolff, Don, 172
Writers & Artists, 254
Wuliger, Frank, 201
Wunsch, Bob, 232
Wyckoff, Craig, 192
Zadeh, Stella , 256
Zeitman, Jerome, 169
Zimmer, Jeremy, 247

■ Index to New York Agents

Adams, Bret, 168
Agency for the Performing Arts, 171
Alessi, Anna Maria, 171
APA, 171
Aspland, Dennis, 211
Beha, Tex, 224
Bernstein, Shirley, 226
Buchwald & Associates, 181
Carver, Bill, 254, 255
Ching, Traci, 181
Cohn, Sam, 202
DGRW, 22, 24, 25, 69
Donaghey, Bob, 245
Douglas, Barry, 22, 24, 25, 61, 69, 187
Duva, Robert, 191
Duva-Flack, 191
Epstein, Gary, 193
Epstein/Wyckoff & Associates, 193
Fifi Oscard Agency, 221
Flack, Elin, 191
Gersh Agency New York, 197
Gorman, Fred, 187
Guc, David, 197
Gwiazola, Ron, 235
Hardin, Mary, 168
Helen Merrill, 220
Hudson, Scott, 254, 255
ICM, 202
ICM/International Creative Management , 202
Joyce Ketay, 207
Ketay, Joyce, 206
Lantz Office, 211
Lantz, Robby, 211

Malcolm, Robert, 173
Meagher, Mary, 197
Merrill, Helen, 220
Mulert, Carl, 206
Oscard, Fifi, 221
paradigm, 225
Paramuse Artists Associates, 226
Rosenstone, Howard, 235
Rosenstone/Wender, 235
Rothacker & Wilhelm, Inc., 187
Rothacker, Flo, 187
Talent East, 245
Wender, Phyllis, 235
Wilhelm, Jim, 187
William Morris Agency, 218
Yoselow, Scott, 197

◼ Index to Directors

Abbott, George, 8

Allen, Woody, 26

Altman, Robert, 66

Arau, Alphonso, 137

Arkush, Allan, 49

Bartel, Paul, 72

Bellisario, Donald, 178

Bigelow, Katherine, 71

Boyd, Julianne, 18

Brest, Martin, 70, 71

Brooks, Mel, 5

Burrows, James, 178

Cameron, James, 9, 48, 139

Capra, Frank, 8

Carpenter, John, 71

Cassavettes, John, 26

Charles, Glen, 178

Cochran, Stacy, 71, 85

Coen, Joel, 71

Columbus, Chris, 71

Coolidge, Martha, 12, 71

Coppola, Francis, 156

Coppola, Francis Ford, 6, 48, 72

Corman, Roger, 18, 48, 49, 78, 145, 153, 156

Curtiz, Michael, 7

Cypher, Julie, 13, 30, 31

Daniele, Graciela, 17

Dante, Joe, 49

Davis, Andrew, 97

Day, Linda, 50

Dickerson, Ernest, 71

Donaldson, Roger, 39

Donen, Stanley, 8

Ephron, Nora, 13

Ford, John, 8

Foster, Jodie, 13

Frankel, Kenneth, 52, 53, 69

Frankenheimer, John, 6

Franklin, Carl, 70

Glaser, Brian, 71

Goldstone, Jim, 51

Hardy, Ron, 42

Heckerling, Amy, 70, 71

Herskovitz, Marshall, 70

Higgins, Colin, 72

Howard, Ron, 71

Ivory, James, 71

Jarmusch, Jim, 71

Jenkins, Tamara, 42

Jimenez, Neil, 72

Joanou, Phil, 71

Jones, Amy, 48

Karamardian, Lark, 55

Kazan, Elia, 25

King Vidor, 7

Kleiser, Randal, 71

Kretchmer, John, 30, 50-52, 147, 148

Kubrick, Stanley, 8

Lee, Spike, 16, 26, 66, 71

Levinson, Barry, 67, 133

Link, Ron, 153

Lubitsch, Ernst, 7

Lucas, George, 71
Lynch, David, 70
Malik, Terrence, 70
Malle, Louis, 8
Marshall, Penny, 13, 139
Martin, Darnell, 32
Mazursky, Paul, 71
McCoy, Terri, 14
Meadow, Lynn, 38
Milius, John, 71
Mizoguchi, Kenji, 7
Pollack, Sydney, 135, 139
Preminger, Otto, 7
Robbins, Tim, 72
Rocco, Mark, 31
Rodriguez, Robert, 16, 75
Ross, Herbert, 52
Sargent, Joe, 32
Sayles, John, 48
Schrader, Paul, 9, 124
Schulman, Susan, 15, 38
Scorsese, Martin, 66, 71
Seidelman, Susan, 71
Shallat, Lee, 57
Singleton, John, 16, 71
Spheeris, Penelope, 72
Spielberg, Steven, 1, 49, 52, 140
Stanley, Florence, 77
Stone, Oliver, 67, 71
Streisand, Barbra, 13, 67
Swados, Liz, 18
Towne, Robert, 78
Townsend, Robert, 16
Ward, David S., 72
Wenders, Wim, 8

Wilder, Billy, 8
Zaks, Jerry, 61, 79, 93, 97, 147
Zemeckis, Robert, 71, 139
Zinberg, Michael, 75
Zwick, Edward, 70

▰ Index to Everything Else

90-Day Clause, 126, 259
90%-10%, 123
Access, 109
Age, 4
Agent—credentials, 96
Agent—definition, 94
Agent—function, 95
Agent—need, 93
Agents—power shift, 141
Agent—training, 96
AIVF Guide, 66
Art of War, 89
Associate producer, 257
Association of Independent Video & Film, 79
Association of Independent Video & Filmmakers, 65
Association of Women in Entertainment, 80
Attitude, 45
AWE, 80
Below-the-line, 257
Bible, 257
British Alternative Theatre Directory, 83
Buzz, 257
Chanticleer Films—address, 80
Chanticleer Films, 80
Chanticleer Films/The Discovery Program, 80
Cinewomen, 81
Co-producers, 257
Commercial directors, 33
Commitment, 26
Competitions, 65
Conglomerate agents—training, 112
Connected, 257
Connected Film Schools, 70

Coverage, 258
Daily Variety—address, 85
Development, 258
DGA membership, 157
DGA minimums, 157
DGA News—address, 85
DGA Report—minorities, 12
DGA—addresses, 89, 159
Directing commercials, 33
Directing—competition, 19
Director/writer alliances, 60
Discovery Program, 80
Divorce, 126
Does Studying Help?, 67
Don't Wait Until It's Too Late, 129
Dramatists Sourcebook, 84
Education, 112
El Mariachi, 16
Executive producer, 258
Film and Video Festivals, 63
Film Schools That Can Make a Difference, 69
FIVF, 65
Foundation for Independent Video & Film, 79
Franchised Agents, 98
Guilds/Unions, 156
Half-hour, 258
How the Business Really Works, 91
Hurd, Gail Ann, 18
IFP, 81
Independent Features Projects, 81
Independent Film Channel, 66
Industrials, 258
Inexperienced Client, 105
Inspiration, 152
Interactive, 258
International Information, 83
International Theater Institute, 83

International theater resources, 84
Leavetaking, 130
Line producer, 258
Long- form television, 258
Make a home for yourself, 43
Make It Worth An Agent's While To Talk To You, 97
Marjorie Ballentine Studio, 60
Miller, Robin Moran, 60, 62
Minorities and Women, 10
Money, 1
New Dramatists, 82, 258
Organizations, 83
Original British Theater Directory, 83
Other Contenders, 72
Other Kinds of Study, 78
Patience, 115
Performing Arts Yearbook, 84
Play Festivals, 63
Playwrighting—contest resource info, 84
Plugged in, 259
Producer, 259
Query/Query letter, 259
Racism, 15
Reader, 259
Reading List, 86
Ready, 28
Reality, 1
Reel Power, 107, 108, 140
Reference Library, 86
Relationships—director/agent, 119
Rider D, 126, 259
Right festival, 64
S.A.S.E., 260
Size, 108
Spec scripts, 260
Speed, 8
SSD&C—addresses, 89

Stage Directors & Choreographers Foundation, 82
Star agent vs. independent agent, 137
Statistics, 1, 11
Stature, 110
Story Analysts, 260
Subject Matter, 35
Support Groups, 44, 78, 81
Synergistic relationship, 123
Take a Writer to Lunch, 60
Tartikoff, Brandon, 26, 27
Telling/Shopping, 129
Theater Communications Group, 84
Theater Schools, 75
Theater Week—address, 85
Things You Will Want to Consider, 106
Think, 260
Time, 97
Tolins, Jonathan, 61
Too much to expect, 121
Trades, 260
Treatment, 260
Virginity, 28
WGA—addresses, 89
Why Agents?, 93
Women and minorities, 11
Writers Guild of America, 258, 260
Writing as a Second Language, 60
Young White Boys Club, 4